Introduction to
Biblical Studies

D0483576

The Cassell Biblical Studies Series

The Cassell Biblical Studies Series is aimed at those taking a course of biblical studies. Developed for the use of those embarking on theological and ministerial education, it is equally helpful in local church situations, and for lay people confused by apparently conflicting approaches to the Scriptures.

Students of biblical studies today will encounter a diversity of inter-pretive positions. Their teachers will – inevitably – lean towards some positions in preference to others. This series offers an integrated approach to the Bible which recognizes this diversity, but helps readers to understand it, and to work towards some kind of unity within it.

This is an ecumenical series, written by Roman Catholics and Protestants. The writers are all professionally engaged in the teaching of biblical studies in theological and ministerial education. The books are the product of that experience, and it is the intention of the editor, Dr Steve Moyise, that their contents should be tested on this exacting audience.

Introduction to Biblical Studies, by Series Editor Steve Moyise, is the first book in the series.

FORTHCOMING TITLES INCLUDE:

The Significance of the Pentateuch
Gillian Sumner
Historical Israel, Biblical Israel
Mary Mills

FURTHER TITLES:

Jesus and the Gospels
Women and the Bible

Introduction to Biblical Studies

STEVE MOYISE

Foreword by Frances Young

CASSELL

Cassell
Wellington House, 125 Strand, London WC2R 0BB
PO Box 605, Herndon, VA 20172

First published 1998

British Library Cataloguing-in-Publication Data
A catalogue record for this book is available from the British Library.

ISBN 0–304–70091–6

Designed by Geoff Green
Typeset by Geoff Green Book Design
Printed and bound in Great Britain by
Biddles Ltd, Guildford and King's Lynn

Contents

Foreword

One of the most persistent biblical motifs is that of the journey – Abraham leaving Ur, Moses leading the Exodus, exiles returning to Zion, Jesus having nowhere to lay his head and setting his face towards Jerusalem. The journey is not always 'literal', becoming a potent image as Christians see themselves as strangers in an alien land, journeying to heaven where they have their true citizenship.

Like the Bible itself, this book invites the reader to set out on a journey. I commend this book and the journey on which it will take you, and I commend it to you especially if you are nervous of venturing into the area it travels through. For this guide understands your anxiety and offers encouragement which dissolves the sense of threat.

The starting-place is where many Christians are, sure that the Bible is the word of God, but liable to be confused by casual confrontations with what seem to us to be puzzles or even absurdities. The marks of this guidebook are down-to-earth commonsense and well-grounded acquaintance with the terrain. The journey retraces the steps of some 200 years of scholarly exploration. Stage by stage we are led into the significance of each approach to biblical interpretation, and this is succinctly demonstrated with neatly chosen examples.

But the ultimate conclusion is that there are many journeys, and they are not all the same. For the key focus must be on how readers are affected by the Bible, how they are changed, how God can use the Bible to speak in different situations. Where once map-makers tried to produce one objective outline, one accurate plan of what it meant in the past, now people are ready to recognize the contribution of many different approaches and the value of by-paths, to acknowledge the variety and indeterminacy of readers and readings and so the certainty of surprises, and to challenge the presumption of any who try to pin down the possibilities of a God beyond comprehension communicating with each in their own language. The miracle is that the same one Bible in its many versions has myriad capacities for that end.

So good journeying, and may you go far!

Frances Young
July 1997

Abbreviations

GNB	Good News Bible
JB	Jerusalem Bible
KJV	King James Bible
NEB	New English Bible
NIV	New International Version
NRSV	New Revised Standard Version
RSV	Revised Standard Version

1

God and the Bible

I was in a church once when the reading for the day happened to be one of the Old Testament genealogies. It wasn't long before the reader realized that he should have practised at home! Each of the Hebrew names required several attempts and, even then, it was not all that close to the words we had in front of us. As a result, the reader became flustered and so coughed and spluttered his way through the reading. It took over five minutes! When he had finally finished, he solemnly closed the Bible, looked at the congregation and uttered the traditional words: 'This is the word of the Lord.' At which the congregation immediately burst out laughing. In part this was a reaction to the tension created by the man's discomfort. But it was also about calling such an odd and seemingly irrelevant passage the 'word of the Lord'.

Most Christians read the Bible because they think that it will somehow bring them closer to God or help them grow in their Christian faith. This book called the Bible is not simply human opinion; it is the 'word of God'. Christians claim this on the authority of Jesus himself. For example, in Mark 7:13, Jesus criticizes the Pharisees' adherence to custom because by it they are 'making void the word of God'. In the Sermon on the Mount, we read that 'until heaven and earth pass away, not one letter, not one stroke of a letter, will pass from the law until all is accomplished' (Matt 5:18). And at the end of Luke's Gospel, Jesus tells his disciples: 'These are my words that I spoke to you while I was still with you – that everything written about me in the law of Moses, the prophets, and the psalms must be fulfilled' (Luke 24:44).

It is a view that is summarized in 2 Timothy 3:16–17: 'All scripture is inspired by God and is useful for teaching, for reproof, for correction, and for training in righteousness, so that everyone who belongs to God may be proficient, equipped for every good work.' The word translated 'inspired' is a compound word (*theo-pneustos*) meaning

'God-breathed' (so NIV). It is not clear if this refers to the way that Scripture came about or to its character. But what it does say is that Scripture is somehow connected with God and has an important function. By means of teaching, reproof, correction and training in righteousness, it prepares people for Christian service. It gives them what they need to be 'proficient, equipped for every good work'.

Both of these quotations are of course referring to what Christians call the Old Testament, that is, those Scriptures which were written before the time of Christ (BC). However, the authors would have been puzzled by our reference to the 'Old Testament' because the 'New Testament' had not yet been written. It would be many years before the Gospels, Acts, Epistles and Revelation were collected together and put alongside the (OT) Scriptures to form one Holy Bible. In recognition of this, and the fact that the Jewish people did not cease to exist once the Church was born, most modern writers now use the abbreviation BCE (Before the Common Era) and CE (Common Era) in preference to BC and AD, and this will be our practice. John Goldingay (*Models for Scripture*, 1994) would also prefer to talk of First and Second Testaments instead of 'Old Testament' and 'New Testament' but here we will stick with conventional usage.

Though it was some time before the New Testament books were collected together to form a canon of Scripture, there is an interesting passage in 2 Peter 3:15–16, which refers to Paul's letters. It is gratifying to know that they were hard to understand even in the first century but the reason for quoting it is the way that it associates Paul's letters with 'the other Scriptures'. The author of 2 Peter says: 'So also our beloved brother Paul wrote to you according to the wisdom given him, speaking of this as he does in all his letters. There are some things in them hard to understand, which the ignorant and unstable twist to their own destruction, as they do the other scriptures.' The use of the word 'other' here appears to put Paul's letters on the same level as those Old Testament books which the author regarded as Scripture.

More texts could be quoted (see especially 2 Pet 1:19–21 and Ps 119) but the above is sufficient to show that the Christian claim that the Bible is the 'word of God' is grounded in the Bible itself. And this is acknowledged in most churches when a reading from the Bible is followed by an acclamation such as 'This is the word of the Lord'. There cannot be many Christians who categorically deny that the Bible has anything to do with God. But Christians do differ on what they believe to be the implications of this. For example, what does the Bible give us (or do for us) that 'mere' human writings do not or cannot? The following have been suggested:

'The Bible gives us knowledge'

As the 'word of God', some would suggest that the primary function of the Bible is to tell us things that we could not otherwise know. For example, some think it can tell us about the creation of the world, even though there were clearly no witnesses to record it (Gen 1). Some think it is only through the Bible that we can find out about angels, the devil and other spiritual forces which cannot be seen (Job 1 – 2). Some even think that the Bible gives us a detailed plan of how the world is going to end (some even try to predict the date). And on a more mundane level, when historians point out that Moses could not have written about his own death (Deut 34), proponents of this view simply declare that God revealed it to him. In other words, unlike any human writing, which is necessarily limited to the knowledge and experience of the author, the Bible comes directly from God and can therefore tell us things that we could not otherwise know.

Now few would wish to deny that the Bible might sometimes function like this but it is a view more usually associated with 'fundamentalism' and 'taking the Bible literally'. Some Christians would prefer to reserve the word 'fundamentalism' for those who believe in the 'fundamentals' of the faith but I will follow popular usage here. Fundamentalists believe that the 'literal' meaning is the only meaning. They see themselves at war with modern culture (modernity), which they believe to be anti-Christian, in both morality and doctrine. Thus when science proposes theories about our origins that differ from the six-day creation of Genesis, science is clearly wrong. It has overreached itself, putting its trust in human wisdom rather than the 'word of God'.

The clash between such views and the growth of biblical criticism will be described in the next chapter but it will be useful to highlight some of the pitfalls now. A moment's reflection will show that each of the books of the Bible has its own particular style. Leviticus is not like Psalms. Paul's letters are not like the Gospels. Kings and Chronicles are not like Revelation. Some New Testament writers use a wide vocabulary and a good Greek style (Luke, Hebrews). Others are more limited in their abilities (Mark) and some even ignore grammatical rules (Revelation, though some think this is done on purpose). Whatever the mechanism which led to the writing of Scripture, it clearly did not bypass the personalities of its human authors.

Indeed, the rich use of parables and figures of speech by Jesus should have made it clear that not everything in the Bible is to be taken literally. If I go down to my local garden shop and purchase some mustard seeds, I have not thereby gained the kingdom of God. In the parable of the mustard seed (Mark 4:30–32), Jesus is comparing some aspect of the kingdom (presumably its growth) to some aspect of a mustard seed. The hearer (and now the reader) is invited to ponder what Jesus was trying to convey. This is no more 'liberal' than recognizing that expressions like 'it's miles away' or 'I'm starving' are figures of speech. The question of whether a particular Bible passage is to be taken literally has to be considered on its merits: its literal veracity cannot simply be assumed because it is in the Bible. Language does not work like that.

There is an amusing story in Mark 8:14–21, where the disciples have forgotten to bring bread for their journey. Later, Jesus warns them to 'beware of the yeast of the Pharisees', which they take to be a rebuke for not bringing any bread. One can almost hear the exasperation in Jesus' voice as he says to them: 'Why are you talking about having no bread? Do you still not perceive or understand? Are your hearts hardened? Do you have eyes, and fail to see? Do you have ears, and fail to hear?' (8:17–18). In other words, they were expected to discern that 'yeast' is a figure of speech for the way that evil or malice spreads. Jesus was not referring to loaves of bread. One can pass an amusing hour with a concordance locating all the verses that are not meant to be taken literally. For example, we are told that 'the eyes of the Lord are everywhere'. A rather gruesome picture if taken literally!

More seriously, it must be recognized that we cannot simply turn to a passage of Scripture and declare 'This is the word of God – I must obey it'. Consider, for example, the end of Psalm 137 (often omitted when read in church): 'Happy shall they be who take your little ones and dash them against the rock!' Now in what sense is this verse true? And in what sense should it be obeyed? The first question is difficult and involves appreciating something of the historical situation and something of the type of language being used. As an expression of extreme grief (this is what the Babylonians had done to Israel), it is understandable (though not commendable). The second question, however, must be answered with an emphatic negative! Jesus taught us to pray for our enemies, not dash their children against the rocks. Taken literally, this verse is not simply mistaken, it is monstrous. But taken as an exaggerated expression (known as hyperbole) of grief, it is understandable. Indeed, one of the reasons that the Psalms are so popular is that they manage to put into words the whole range of human feelings (from joy and peace to anger and vengeance) and offer them to God in worship. But they are certainly not commands to be obeyed!

Even something as seemingly clear-cut as the command 'You shall not kill' (Exod 20:13, RSV) requires interpretation. Does it apply to animals? Does it forbid capital punishment? What about war? Should all Christians be pacifists? Though there is something appealing (for some) about a form of Christianity that always deals in clear-cut answers, one cannot avoid questions of interpretation. Indeed, the Bible portrays God as commanding the killing of animals (for sacrifice), criminals (for a range of offences) and the Canaanites (to provide Israel with a promised land). Our generation has seen horrific deeds done in the name of God, some of which made appeal to passages like these. The principle of 'read the Bible, obey the Bible' is not only simplistic, it is also very dangerous.

'The Bible shows us how to live'

Many Christians feel that the Bible is not there to give information to the curious but to teach us how to live. Most of the Bible does not consist of doctrine but of stories, focusing on particular individuals. For example, Abraham and his descendants dominate the book of Genesis; Moses is the focus of Exodus; David is the key figure in Samuel and Kings; the Gospels are about Jesus; Peter and Paul are the central figures in Acts. Though separated by thousands of years, such stories give us glimpses of 'people living before God'. We are not the first generation to try and be faithful to God. There is much to learn from those that have gone before us.

Furthermore, what many find valuable about the biblical stories is that they seldom try to hide the character's weaknesses. They do not give us a selection of 'plaster saints'. For example, Abraham puts his wife in jeopardy by telling the king that she is his sister (Gen 20:2). Moses makes excuses for not doing what God wants (Exod 4:1). David commits adultery and then arranges for the husband to die (2 Sam 11:15). Peter and Paul fall out over the issue of eating with Gentiles (Gal 2:11). And even Jesus, though never presented as actually sinning, would prefer some other way of doing God's will if it is at all possible (Mark 14:36) and, according to Matthew and Mark, ends his life with the cry: 'My God, my God, why have you forsaken me?' (Matt 27:46; Mark 15:34).

Stories do not function by offering us a set of doctrines. There is something about a good story which has the potential to inspire, warn, encourage or challenge. It offers us a vision of what life or faith could become. As we identify with particular characters, our horizons are expanded. Why shouldn't we have a faith like Abraham or Ruth or Paul or Mary? They were in touch with the same God as we are. On this view then, the Bible is mainly a collection of stories about people 'living before God', which can inspire us to do likewise. It is of course possible that certain stories may *imply* certain doctrines (the book of Jonah is certainly saying something about the love of God). But that is not their primary function. Stories operate on a different level, as we shall see in Chapter 4.

'The Bible reveals the way of salvation'

Without denying the above, some would wish to narrow the focus. What holds the diverse literature of the Bible together is the story of salvation, from Genesis to Revelation. It does not just offer principles on how to live. Rather, through the long history of Israel to the coming of Christ, the Bible reveals a plan of salvation. As the author of Hebrews put it: 'Long ago God spoke to our ancestors in many and various ways by the prophets, but in these last days he has spoken to us by a Son' (1:1–2). Thus while we might be able to learn something from every part of the Bible, not every passage is of equal importance.

Accordingly, we read in the New Testament of heated debates about whether the coming of Christ implies that the food laws or the practice of circumcision are still in force (see Acts 15, Gal 2, Rom 14). Paul's opinion that such laws should not be imposed on Gentiles is extremely significant, for the Old Testament (see Gen 17) is quite adamant that they are both mandatory and binding. But Paul declares in Galatians 5:6 that 'in Christ Jesus neither circumcision nor uncircumcision counts for anything'. On what basis can he decide that certain scriptural commandments are no longer to be obeyed? The answer is complex (as we shall see in Chapter 7) but clearly has something to do with the revelation of Christ. Paul now reads the (OT) Scriptures in a new light (2 Cor 3:15–16). Revelation is not static in the Bible, as John 16:13 makes clear: 'When the Spirit of truth comes, he will guide you into all the truth; for he will not speak on his own, but will speak whatever he hears, and he will declare to you the things that are to come.'

'The Bible reveals God'

The goal of reading the Bible is not to obtain information about God or even about the story of salvation; the goal of reading the Bible is to experience the God that the Bible talks about. On this view, the Bible is called the 'word of God' not because it was dictated by God but because these (very) human words are somehow able to mediate God's presence. Consider, for example, Isaiah's vision of God, recorded in Isaiah 6:1–5:

In the year that King Uzziah died, I saw the Lord sitting on a throne, high and lofty; and the hem of his robe filled the temple. Seraphs were in attendance above him; each had six wings: with two they covered their faces, and with two they covered their feet, and with two they flew. And one called to another and said:

'Holy, holy, holy is the Lord of hosts; the whole earth is full of his glory.'

The pivots on the thresholds shook at the voices of those who called, and the house filled with smoke. And I said: 'Woe is me! I am lost, for I am a man of unclean lips, and I live among a people of unclean lips; yet my eyes have seen the King, the Lord of hosts!'

This text could be analysed to see what doctrine it might imply. It clearly speaks of the holiness of God. Or we could try and use it as an example of 'living before God'. Perhaps we should acknowledge our sins more often. But both of these fall short of experiencing the God that Isaiah experienced. In other words, Isaiah had a revelation or experience of God; we have an account of that experience in the Bible. The two are not identical, as can be seen from the countless number of people who have read this passage and been completely unmoved by it. Something has to happen for the words of Scripture to come alive.

Many Christians believe that this is the aim of reading the Bible. Whether by study or prayer, discussion or meditation, the Bible can be the vehicle for an experience of God. As the author of Hebrews put it, 'the word of God is living and active, sharper than any two-edged sword, piercing until it divides soul from spirit, joints from marrow; it is able to judge the thoughts and intentions of the heart' (4:12). My own conversion to Christianity was through reading Luke's Gospel. I was an undergraduate student in London and had never read the Bible or gone to church in my life. One day, two evangelists knocked on my door and tried to convert me. I was not interested but, for some reason, they came back (weekly!). Eventually, they offered me a challenge. Read Luke's Gospel in a modern version and decide for yourself. It was some months before I took up the challenge (hiding the Bible they had lent me under my bed lest any of my friends should spot it) but when I did, something totally unexpected happened. The words on the page became so real that I could almost hear Jesus calling me, as if I were one of the first disciples. And like those in the story, I felt compelled to follow him.

However, I would be less than honest if I were to imply that this is always my experience of reading the Bible. Sometimes it seems very dull. Some passages seem so obscure that it is hard to see any relevance in them at all. And some are so annoying that it is hard to understand how they got there in the first place! I have come to believe that inspiration ('God-breathed') is more to do with what God does with the text than what it supposedly guarantees. And this is the hub of the matter for me. Whatever our beliefs about inspiration, they have got to do justice to what we actually find in the Bible. For example, there is no point maintaining that, because the Bible is the 'word of God', everything must be taken literally. Such a view leads to absurdities. Nor (in my opinion) can we hold the view that inspiration guarantees that every writer agrees with every other writer. As we shall see in the next chapter, the growth of historical criticism has made this conclusion extremely unlikely.

So how should we understand the human and the divine in the Bible? Such a question is not of course unique. Christian theology has found the same sort of dilemma when discussing the person of Christ, the Christian Church or the sacraments. In each case, scholars have wanted to assert that there is both a human element and a divine element. But how are they related?

The person of Christ

From the Gospel stories, Jesus was clearly a human being who ate, drank, slept, grew tired, prayed, discussed and died. But Christianity also claims that, in this human life, God was incarnate. As the author of the Fourth Gospel says: 'In the beginning was the Word, and the Word was with God, and the Word was God' (John 1:1). Many of the (so-called) heresies in the Church can be put down to a wrong emphasis on one or other of these aspects. For example, the 'docetists' argued that if Jesus was God, then he must have been all-powerful, even as a child. But in response, others declared that unless Jesus shared the same weaknesses and limitations of childhood (and adulthood) that we do, then he cannot be regarded as fully human. It took centuries of debate to arrive at a formula which did justice to both aspects (Council of Chalcedon, 451 CE) and even that leaves many questions unanswered.

The Church

The Church is often called the 'body of Christ' but I am not sure that Christ can be held responsible for everything the Church does! On the one hand, it is a 'spiritual house... a holy priesthood' (1 Pet 2:5). But on the other, it is plagued by divisions (1 Cor 1 – 3), immorality (1 Cor 5) and disorder (1 Cor 12 – 14). Indeed, it is often difficult to see how the divine could be related to such an institution at all. The answer is presumably 'by grace', that somehow our all too human efforts to be Church are transformed into something pleasing to God. Is this how it is with the Bible, that these very human writings ('dash them against the rock') can 'by grace' become vehicles for revelation? Or is it closer to the analogy of the person of Christ, who may have shown human weakness but whom tradition regards as sinless. In other words, the Bible might reflect the limitations of its authors (e.g. science) but is never actually wrong.

The sacraments

During a service of Holy Communion (Eucharist, Lord's Supper), words such as 'the body of Christ' and 'the blood of Christ' are associated with ordinary bread and wine. There are great debates as to what happens (if anything) to the bread and wine during the consecration but most Christians accept that 'taking communion' is significantly different from taking coffee and biscuits after the service. In some way or another, ordinary things become the vehicle for God's grace. Whether this is a helpful analogy for how the human words of the Bible can become the 'living word' will depend on one's understanding of the sacraments. But the analogy does at least draw attention to the fact that the biblical writings do not differ from other writings in formal terms (grammar, vocabulary, style, etc.). They are very human writings, as can be seen from Paul's offhand comment in Galatians 5:12 ('I wish those who unsettle you would castrate themselves!'). And for some readers (perhaps many) they never become anything more than this. But other readers testify to the life-changing power of the Bible, just as some claim to experience God in the sacraments.

Conclusion

Many debates about interpretation are conducted from two opposing camps. There are those that regard certain types of questions (e.g. 'Did Jesus say these actual words?' or 'Did Israel really cross the Red Sea?') as incompatible with belief in the absolute truth of Scripture. If the Bible is the 'word of God', then God would not have allowed mistakes. Hence if the Gospel writers say Jesus said something, then he did. It is this that separates the Bible from all other writings. Indeed, even to ask such questions is to put oneself above the Bible and biblical criticism is precisely that – unbelievers criticizing the Bible.

On the other hand, some think that this effectively denies that the

Bible was written by human beings. It assumes that it somehow 'dropped from the sky' or was dictated 'word for word'. Claims that the Bible is the unchallengeable word of God put all the emphasis on the divine side, and so this second camp chooses to emphasize the 'humanness' of the writings. The authors were people of their time. They shared in the culture and beliefs of their time and could not have written about things which were only discovered centuries later. Thus it is absurd to try and reconcile Genesis with modern theories of the universe. It is clear (so it is argued) that the biblical writers accepted the science of their day. And any responsible study of the Bible must recognize this.

However, it will be clear as we proceed that this latter position can be just as dogmatic as the former. What has seemed obvious and irrefutable to one generation of scholars has been challenged by the next. Indeed, many of the approaches that we shall mention arose because of the inadequacies of those that had gone before. This is important to bear in mind, for when I am discussing a particular approach, I shall endeavour to present it in as positive a light as possible. My aim is to convey something of the rationale of the approach and its contribution to our understanding of the Bible. You may initially feel that I have swallowed the approach 'hook, line and sinker' but a critique will follow, usually in the subsequent chapters. However, I do believe that each approach has something important to say and is therefore worth trying to understand.

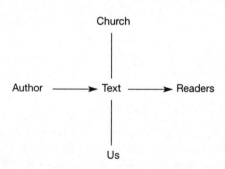

The first approach we shall look at is *historical criticism*. Prior to the eighteenth century, the meaning of the Bible was largely in the hands of the church hierarchy. The Bible meant what the church authorities told you it meant and there was very little that the ordinary person could do about it. However, the period known as 'the Enlightenment' (late seventeenth century until recently) did offer such a challenge.

It resented the idea that the Church was accountable to no one and suggested that truth should be open to public debate. Setting aside centuries of dogma, it began an historical quest to discover what the original authors meant and what the original readers would have understood. In terms of a diagram, it drew attention away from the vertical dimension of *Church–Text–Us* by emphasizing the importance of the horizontal or historical dimension. Before the books of the Bible were Ecclesiastical Scripture, they were real communication between an author and a set of readers. Historical criticism set out to learn all it could about the original circumstances of these writings. The results were to completely change the way that modern people look at the Bible.

FURTHER READING

Raymond F. Collins offers a useful survey of the doctrine of inspiration in ch. 65 of *The New Jerome Biblical Commentary* (Geoffrey Chapman, 1989). This is the single most useful purchase for someone beginning a course in biblical studies. As well as a commentary on all the books of the Bible (including what Protestants call the Apocrypha), there are 19 additional chapters covering such issues as Old and New Testament Criticism, Inspiration and Canon, Text and Versions, Archaeology and History, Dead Sea Scrolls, Old and New Testament Thought and many others. Evangelical students will probably want to supplement this with the two excellent Bible dictionaries from Inter-Varsity Press: *Dictionary of Paul and His Letters* (ed. G. F. Hawthorne, R. P. Martin, D. G. Reid, 1993) and *Dictionary of Jesus and the Gospels* (ed. J. B. Green, S. McKnight, I. H. Marshall, 1992).

James Barr's *The Bible in the Modern World* (SCM/Harper, 1973) is a good introduction to the issues facing a doctrine of inspiration today. He examines the way that inspiration and authority have been understood in the past; considers the challenges posed by the Enlightenment; and looks at the difference between 'event and interpretation', 'word and meaning', 'letter and spirit'. More extensive and from a broadly evangelical point of view is John Goldingay's *Models for Scripture* (Eerdmans/Paternoster, 1994). He points out that the Bible does sometimes speak of God dictating words to human authors (Exod 32:16, Rev 1:11) and prophets 'hear' what God wants them to say (Hos 1:1, Joel 1:1). But he also suggests that it is a mistake to impose such a model on the Bible as a whole. For example, Luke decides 'after investigating everything carefully from the very first, to write an orderly account' (Luke 1:3). Paul can say 'I have no command of the Lord, but I give my opinion' (1 Cor 7:25). And Jeremiah can complain (to God) about how God has treated him (Jer 20:7–18). Goldingay considers a variety of 'models' of inspiration, including parallels with the incarnation, the Spirit's involvement in the Church, creative inspiration, the sacraments and God's acts in history. Students of all persuasions will find something helpful in this very reasonably priced book.

2

The Bible and history

One of the chief features of the modern world is its sense of history. We are aware that we think and live in ways that are very different from ancient peoples. This is well illustrated by the interpretation offered by Augustine (perhaps the greatest theologian the Church has ever known) of the parable of the Good Samaritan. He explains:

> *A certain man went down from Jerusalem to Jericho;* Adam himself is meant; *Jerusalem* is the heavenly city of peace, from whose blessedness Adam fell; *Jericho* means the moon, and signifies our mortality, because it is born, waxes, wanes, and dies. *Thieves* are the devil and his angels. *Who stripped him,* namely, of his immortality; *and beat him,* by persuading him to sin; *and left him half-dead,* because in so far as man can understand and know God, he lives, but in so far as he is wasted and oppressed by sin, he is dead; he is therefore called *half-dead.* The *priest and Levite...* signify the priesthood and ministry of the *Old Testament,* which could profit nothing for salvation. *Samaritan* means Guardian, and therefore the Lord Himself is signified by this name... being *set upon the beast* is belief in the incarnation of Christ. The *inn* is the Church, where travellers returning to their heavenly country are refreshed after pilgrimage... The *two pence* are either the two precepts of love, or the promise of this life and of that which is to come. The *innkeeper* is the Apostle (Paul)...[1]

Whatever value this explanation had in terms of contemporary relevance, what is most apparent to any modern reader is that Jesus could not possibly have meant this. The simple story told by Jesus in order to answer the lawyer's question 'who is my neighbour?' (Luke 10:29) has been turned into an allegory of Christian doctrine. And this is not an isolated example. This is how most of the parables were interpreted until the modern period. The question of what Jesus meant by a parable was secondary to what it signified in the commentator's own day. Thus some took the two pence as signifying the sacraments of baptism and eucharist. Why? Because that is what nourishes the Christian in the Church (inn) until Jesus returns.

Historical criticism tries to discover the circumstances behind each of the biblical books. It recognizes that, in the first instance, the books were written not to us but to a particular set of readers. For example, Paul's reason for writing what we now call 1 Corinthians is connected with a report from someone called Chloe: 'For it has been reported to me by Chloe's people that there are quarrels among you... each of you says, "I belong to Paul," or "I belong to Apollos," or "I belong to Cephas"' (1:11–12). This letter is not written to you or me. I do not know of anyone in my church or any other church who claims to follow Apollos; yet this is what 1 Corinthians is said to be about. There may well be things that I can learn from it (that is why it was passed on) but it is not addressed to me directly.

Historical criticism seeks to discover the background to the writing. Who was Apollos? What was he doing in Corinth? Did he have a 'party' and, if so, what did it stand for? Some of this might be answered by Acts 18:24: 'Now there came to Ephesus a Jew named Apollos, a native of Alexandria. He was an eloquent man, well-versed in the scriptures.' If this is the same Apollos, it might explain Paul's statements about coming to Corinth not with eloquence or clever words (unlike some!) but determined only to preach Christ crucified (1 Cor 2:1–5). Luther suggested that Apollos was the author of the letter to the Hebrews (it is unsigned) and this has been taken up by Hugh Montefiore (*A Commentary on the Epistle to the Hebrews*, 1964), who further suggests that it was sent to Corinth. This has not won much support but it is an interesting proposal.

The rationale of historical criticism is that meaning always depends on *context*. It is not enough to know what someone said: we need to know the context in which they said it. For example, writing to the Philippian church, Paul is able to give this promise: 'I am confident of this, that the one who began a good work among you will bring it to completion by the day of Jesus Christ' (1:6). It is a promise that many Christians have clung to during difficult times. Even if we fail, God remains true to us; what He started, He will finish. (It is difficult to know what pronoun to use for God. The impersonal 'it' is out of the question; 'he' or 'she' implies a specific gender, while the combined 'he/she' or '(s)he' is clumsy. I have therefore decided to use the capitalized 'He' to mark the fact that the word is not being used in its ordinary human sense. This will be discussed further in Chapter 5.)

In terms of doctrine, this verse in Philippians 1:6 has been used to support the 'eternal security' of the believer. A rather less encouraging statement, however, is found in the letter to the Hebrews:

> For it is impossible to restore again to repentance those who have once been enlightened, and have tasted the heavenly gift, and have shared in the Holy Spirit, and have tasted the goodness of the word of God and the powers of the age to come, and then have fallen away, since on their own they are crucifying again the Son of God and are holding him up to contempt. (6:4–6)

As absolute statements, these appear to be contradictory but, in historical terms, they might be understandable. To a church that is suffering and divided, Paul offers promise and encouragement. Philippians is a letter full of joy and praise. But to a church that is on the point of apostasy, the author of Hebrews issues a stinging rebuke. You do not say to a child playing with an electricity socket 'Isn't it fortunate that God will protect you from electricity?' First, you remove the danger and then talk it out. And there is plenty in Hebrews which might be described as 'talking it out'. Thus the context helps us to appreciate why something was said as well as what was said. And this is necessary before any truth claims (such as whether a Christian can fall from grace) can be evaluated.

Sources of the Bible

Historians depend on sources to reconstruct history. If no one felt an event was worth writing about, it is lost forever (though archaeology may uncover non-written remains, such as evidence of a battle). When we listen to the news, almost every item is immediately followed by its source ('according to a close member of the family'; 'as the football manager said today'). Unsubstantiated claims are soon dismissed. Only that which comes from reliable sources can be used to reconstruct history.

What then are the sources of the Bible? Where did the authors get their information from? Were they reliable sources? These questions were sharply aimed at the Bible during the eighteenth century. And one of the first observations to come to light was that the Pentateuch (the first five books of the Bible) is not the work of a single author. Traditionally, this was thought to be Moses but Deuteronomy 34 contains a record of his death. Are we to believe that God inspired him to write about his own death? Some would answer 'Yes', arguing that if God could cause Moses to predict the coming of a future prophet (Deut 18:15–22), He could certainly cause him to write about his own death. But Deuteronomy 34 does not claim to be prophecy and it does not sound like prophecy. What it sounds like is a later generation paying homage to Moses:

> Then Moses, the servant of the Lord, died there in the land of Moab... He was buried in a valley in the land of Moab, opposite Beth-peor, but no one knows his burial place to this day... Never since has there arisen a prophet in Israel like Moses, whom the Lord knew face to face. (34:5, 6, 10)

The most obvious explanation is that someone thought the stories *about* Moses would not be complete without an account of his death and a tribute to his accomplishments. Furthermore, there are signs of editing in the books themselves. Thus in Genesis 12:6, we are told that 'At that time the Canaanites were in the land'. This is clearly written by someone who is living after Israel had taken over the promised land. Genesis 36:31 says 'These are the kings who reigned in the land of Edom, before any king reigned over the Israelites'. Whoever wrote these words not only knows about Israel's conquest (the theme of Joshua and Judges), he or she also knows about the establishment of the monarchy in Israel (the theme of Samuel and Kings). Who these authors/editors were and when they were working is still a matter of debate but almost all scholars accept that Moses could not have written these comments (just as he could not have written about his own death). Even a scholar as conservative as Edward Young (*An Introduction to the Old Testament*, 1964) says:

> When we affirm that Moses wrote, or that he was the author of, the Pentateuch, we do not mean that he himself necessarily wrote every word. To insist upon this would be unreasonable. Hammurabi was the author of his famous code, but he certainly did not engrave it himself upon the stele. Our Lord was the author of the Sermon upon the Mount, but He did not write it Himself. Milton was the author of *Paradise Lost*, but he did not write it all out by hand.[2]

However, what remains controversial was the observation that Genesis appears to contain not one but two accounts of creation. The first is set out in Genesis 1:1 – 2:4a and describes creation in six days, the climax being the creation of 'male and female' together (1:26–29). After providing a habitable earth, God creates plant life, creatures of sea and air, animals and finally human beings. However, Genesis 2:4b–25 describes the creation of Adam (2:7), then the animals (2:19), and then, because none of these offer suitable companionship for the man, woman is created from Adam's rib (2:21–23).

The difference between these two accounts is not simply that of chronology but outlook and content. Thus, in the first account, God simply utters the word and something comes into being. In the second, God first makes a shape from the dust of the ground and then breathes life into it. In the first, the emphasis is on male and female in the image of God (and hence set apart from the rest of creation). In the second, our proximity to the earth is emphasized by a word play. The Hebrew word for ground is *adamah* and so God makes *adam* from the *adamah*. This connection is lost when we translate *adam* as 'man' (which also introduces gender distinctions). A cumbersome but more accurate rendering would be something like 'from the earth came the earth-creature'. Lastly, throughout Genesis 1:1 – 2:4a, the Hebrew word for God is *elohim* but, in the second story (2:4b–25), it is always the compound form *yahweh elohim* (usually translated 'Lord God').

This is highly significant because the Genesis 2 account ('Adam's rib') has been used to promote subservient (not to say misogynist) roles for women as representing God's will. Though it goes against modern understandings of equality, some Christians argue that Genesis 2 – 3 lays down a hierarchy of being where men are leaders and women are followers. As Eve is told: 'I will greatly increase your pangs in childbearing; in pain you shall bring forth children, yet your desire shall be for your husband, and he shall rule over you' (Gen 3:16). However, if someone wishes to argue that this is how things ought to be today (whether in marriage, society or church leadership), the following ought to be considered:

1. It may be the emphasis in Genesis 2 (though this can be disputed) but it is certainly not the emphasis in Genesis 1. Quite the opposite. The author/editor seems to have gone out of his or her way to stress that male and female were created together in God's image. On what basis does one choose to give priority to the second account?

2. By adding up the genealogical data, Archbishop Ussher (*Annals of the World*, 1658) calculated that, according to the Bible, Adam and Eve were created in 4004 BCE. Modern science (whether astronomy, geology or biology) declares that to be impossible. Indeed, there are indications in Genesis itself that the story is not meant to be taken literally. Thus, after the murder of Abel, Cain fears that wherever he goes, people will molest him (Gen 4:14). But according to the story, Adam and Eve are the only people alive! Now either the author/editor was incredibly stupid and did not realize this glaring error or he or she was not aiming to give a literal account. The critical view is that the story was written to say something about sin and evil, not to give details about our supposed ancestors.

3. Even on the level of the story, gender roles are not how things ought to be (Gen 1 – 2) but the result of the Fall (Gen 3). However, as Romans 5:12–21 points out, Christ has reversed the effects of the Fall. Why then should we insist on gender roles based on the old order? Should we not take Paul's statement in Galatians 3:28 that in Christ 'there is no longer male and female' to be our guide?
4. The most critical question to be faced is whether the stories of Genesis command male dominance (patriarchy) or reflect it. It is well known that much of ancient culture was patriarchal. Do the accounts simply reflect the assumptions of the culture from which they come? Or are they God's blueprint for how things ought to be? The question is clearly of some importance and will be discussed further in Chapter 5.

Another observation was that the styles of the two creation accounts (including the use of different names for God) were seen to reappear in the flood story (Gen 6 – 9). However, in this case, they are not complete accounts placed side by side but appear as alternate paragraphs. The change in the divine name is indicated in the NRSV by using 'God' for *elohim* and 'Lord' for *yahweh*.

6:9 Noah walked with *God*.	
6:12 *God* saw that the earth was corrupt	7:1 Then the *Lord* said to Noah
	7:5 Noah did all the *Lord* had commanded him.
7:9 male and female, went into the ark with Noah, as *God* had com manded Noah.	
7:16a And those who entered, male and female of all flesh, went in as *God* had commanded him.	
	7:16b and the *Lord* shut him in.
	7:22 everything on dry land in whose nostrils was the breath of life died.
8:1 But *God* remembered Noah... And *God* made a wind	
	8:20 Then Noah built an altar to the *Lord*
	8:21 the *Lord* smelled the pleasing odour
9:1 *God* blessed Noah... 'Be fruitful and multiply'	
9.6 for in his own image *God* made humankind.	

What is particularly interesting about this is that, in the 'God' (*elohim*) passages, we see other examples of Genesis 1 language, such as 'God saw' (cf. 1:10), 'male and female' (cf. 1:27), 'be fruitful and multiply' (cf. 1:28) and 'in his own image God made humankind' (cf. 1:27). On the other hand, 7:22 reproduces the characteristic way that Genesis 2 refers to life, namely, 'everything on dry land in whose nostrils was the breath of life' (cf. 2:7). It appears that the author/ editor of Genesis had access to two different sources, written in very different styles. One referred to God as *elohim* and pictured Him as utterly transcendent, able to create by the mere utterance of a word. The other source used the covenant name *yahweh* or *yahweh elohim* (see Exod 6:3) and had a much more immanent view of God (He forms Adam from the dust; He walks in the garden; He closes the door of the ark; He smells the odour).

This theory was then expanded by such scholars as K. H. Graf and given classic exposition by Julius Wellhausen (*Prologomena zur Geschichte Israels*, 1878), whereby the whole of the Pentateuch was thought to be composed of four basic sources, these two (known as J and P) and two others (known as E and D). D was primarily the book of Deuteronomy (*deuteros* = second, *nomos* = law), which repeats many of the laws of Exodus and Leviticus but with some surprising differences. For example, Deuteronomy 5 contains an alternative version of the ten commandments. These mostly agree with Exodus 20 except for the sabbath command (differences in italics):

Exodus 20:8–11	*Deuteronomy 5:12–15*
Remember the sabbath day, and keep it holy.	*Observe* the sabbath day and keep it holy, *as the Lord your God commanded you*. Six days you shall labour and do all your work. But the seventh day is a sabbath to the Lord your God; you shall not do any work – you, or your son or your daughter, *or* your male or female slave, *or your ox or your donkey, or any of* your livestock, *or* the resident alien in your towns, *so that your male and female slave may rest as well as you. Remember that you were a slave in the land of Egypt, and the Lord your God brought you out from there with a mighty hand and an outstretched arm; therefore the Lord your God commanded you to keep the sabbath day.*
Six days you shall labour and do all your work. But the seventh day is a sabbath to the Lord your God; you shall not do any work – you, your son or your daughter, your male or female slave, your livestock, or the alien resident in your towns.	
For in six days the Lord made heaven and earth, the sea, and all that is in them, but rested the seventh day; therefore the Lord blessed the sabbath day and consecrated it.	

Both traditions know that the sabbath was commanded by God but they differ as to the reason. Exodus 20 looks back to the Genesis account and is the version used in our prayer books. It is based on a creation principle. Deuteronomy 5 looks back to the Exodus (it would be strange for modern people to recite these words) and is based on a redemption principle ('God brought you out'). The most plausible explanation for this difference (it was argued) is that they come from different sources (E and D) and have been preserved because the editor(s) did not want to omit anything important. This is why we have two creation accounts, a composite account of the flood and two versions of the ten commandments (actually three, see Exod 34). The picture that was emerging is that the Pentateuch, as we know it, is a collection of material that has grown over the centuries, rather than the work of a single author (including Moses).

However, many scholars went further than this general conclusion and tried to assign each and every verse of the Pentateuch to one of these four sources. This was particularly difficult in those passages where the divine name does not occur at all (e.g. Gen 23, 36 – 37, 47). Instead, such scholars had to look for other signs of editing, such as sudden changes of style or vocabulary, inconsistencies or repetition. For example, consider the story of Joseph's betrayal by his brothers in Genesis 37:

> So Joseph went after his brothers, and found them at Dothan. They saw him from a distance, and before he came near to them, they conspired to kill him. They said to one another, 'Here comes this dreamer. Come now, let us kill him and throw him into one of the pits; then we shall say that a wild animal has devoured him, and we shall see what will become of his dreams.' But when *Reuben* heard it, he delivered him out of their hands, saying, 'Let us not take his life.' *Reuben* said to them, 'Shed no blood; throw him into this pit here in the wilderness, but lay no hand on him' – that he might rescue him out of their hand and restore him to his father. So when Joseph came to his brothers, they stripped him of his robe, the long robe with sleeves that he wore; and they took him and threw him into a pit. The pit was empty; there was no water in it. Then they sat down to eat; and looking up they saw a caravan of Ishmaelites coming from Gilead, with their camels carrying gum, balm, and resin, on their way to carry it down to Egypt. Then Judah said to his brothers, 'What profit is it if we kill our brother and conceal his blood? Come, let us sell him to the Ishmaelites, and not lay our hands on him, for he is our brother, our own flesh.' And his brothers agreed. When some Midianite traders passed by, they drew Joseph up, lifting him out of the pit, and sold him to the Ishmaelites for twenty pieces of silver.

And they took Joseph to Egypt. When Reuben returned to the pit and saw that Joseph was not in the pit, he tore his clothes. He returned to his brothers, and said, 'The boy is gone; and I, where can I turn?' (Gen 37:17b–30)

Though the double mention of Reuben at the beginning is a little inelegant, the story makes sense up until Judah's suggestion that they sell Joseph to the Ishmaelites rather than kill him. This is odd because we have just been told that the brothers decided not to kill him; that is why he is in the pit. Furthermore, the mention of the Midianites is puzzling. The brothers see a caravan of Ishmaelites but 'when some Midianite traders passed by, they drew Joseph up, lifting him out of the pit, and sold him to the Ishmaelites'. Are we to understand that the Midianite traders acted as brokers or is 'Midianite' an alternative way of referring to an 'Ishmaelite'? And then there is Reuben himself. At the beginning of the story, he acts to save Joseph by suggesting the pit rather than killing him. Then we are told that 'they sat down to eat; and looking up they saw a caravan of Ishmaelites'. But this cannot have included Reuben, or the ending ('When Reuben returned') makes no sense. Thus we must assume that having persuaded the brothers to do as he suggested, he went off somewhere, though there is no hint of this in the text.

This unevenness is explained by S. R. Driver (*The Book of Genesis*, 1904) by reference to sources. The editor had at his disposal two versions of Joseph's betrayal, one where Judah takes the lead and one where it is Reuben who acts to save Joseph. If we separate the story into these sources, we find that:

> In J, *Judah* takes the lead: he dissuades his other brethren from carrying out their purpose, and induces them to sell Joseph to a caravan of *Ishmaelites*, who happened to be passing by on their way from Gilead into Egypt; and the Ishmaelites, upon their arrival in Egypt, sell him as a slave to an Egyptian of rank (xxxix.1). In E, *Reuben* takes the lead, and dissuades the other brethren from carrying out their plan: at his suggestion, they cast Joseph into a pit, and *Midianite* traders, passing by, draw him up out of the pit, while his brethren are at their meal, and sell him in Egypt to Potiphar.[3]

There are two main difficulties with this. The first is that in order to separate the story into two sources, Driver has to assume that one of the early references to 'Reuben' originally read 'Judah'. But any theory that requires us to change the primary data is bound to appear suspect. It is not impossible; such changes do occur in textual transmission, as we shall see in Chapter 6. But without specific textual support, we shall require firm evidence from elsewhere before we agree that the text *must* have read 'Judah'. Second, even if it is true that the editor is drawing on ancient sources, what is the evidence that the 'Judah' story comes from the same source that gave us the second creation account? It does not use *yahweh elohim* since it does not speak of God at all. And since it does not speak of God at all, it cannot be argued that its outlook is immanent rather than transcendent.

Indeed, this is the basic difficulty with the JEDP hypothesis. There is general agreement that the Pentateuch draws on various sources and has been edited over a period of time. But whether these can be reconstructed or indeed whether it is right to talk of them as documents (as opposed to traditions) is doubtful. Many scholars still find it useful to speak of a J or a P tradition but very few accept the detailed reconstructions of Wellhausen and Driver. Conservative scholars such as Young take this as a victory for the traditional view:

> The Pentateuch exhibits an inner plan and structure that betray a great mind. Who, better than Moses, could have produced such a work? More than two hundred years of exhaustive study have been unable to produce a satisfactory substitute for the time-honoured biblical view that Moses himself was the human author of the Law. Hence, we cannot do better than to regard the Pentateuch as the product of the great lawgiver of Israel.[4]

The majority of scholars, however, do not find this accords with the facts. The signs of editing are clearly present in the text. If the original JEDP theory is unsatisfactory, it is not because the evidence points to a single author but because it points to a much more complicated process than the pasting together of four fixed documents.

The Gospels

In the New Testament, the big question was the relationship between the Gospels. For example, how did Jesus face death? According to Mark, Jesus utters a cry of despair: 'My God, my God, why have you forsaken me?' (15:34). No other words are recorded by Mark, leaving nothing to offset the sombre nature of the whole event. But John offers a different picture. In John 19, Jesus utters three sayings from the cross. The first is an expression of concern for his soon-to-be bereaved mother (19:26–27). The second is to express his thirst (19:28), which we are immediately told was to fulfil Scripture. And third, Jesus' final words are 'It is finished' (19:30). There are no signs of despair or questioning God or wondering what is happening. Jesus is in perfect control. He is returning from whence he came.

An historian is bound to ask which of these accounts is closest to what actually happened. Did Jesus end his life with a despairing question or a confident assertion? Previously, questions of this sort were answered by trying to harmonize the accounts. Everything in the Gospels is true and so must somehow fit together. But the problem is far more complex than trying to imagine a scenario where Jesus experiences both despair (Mark) and assurance (John). Read on their own, each Gospel is clearly trying to give a different impression. Indeed, if Jesus ultimately left this life with the confident assurance that John suggests, then one can only describe Mark as perverse in omitting all mention of it.

What of the other Gospels? Reading Mark and John side by side reveals almost no verbal parallels. They appear to come from quite different sources. But Matthew and Luke are often very similar to Mark (they are known as the 'Synoptic' Gospels because they can be arranged in a synopsis). Consider, for example, how they describe the events that follow Jesus' death:

Matthew 27:45, 51	*Mark 15:33, 38*	*Luke 23:44, 45*
From noon on, darkness came over the whole land until three in the afternoon...	When it was noon, darkness came over the whole land until three in the afternoon...	It was now about noon, and darkness came over the whole land until three in the afternoon...
At that moment the curtain of the temple was torn in two, from top to bottom.	And the curtain of the temple was torn in two, from top to bottom.	and the curtain of the temple was torn in two.

As for the crucifixion scene, Matthew agrees with Mark that the last words of Jesus were 'My God, my God, why have you forsaken me?' (27:46). But Luke is more like John in recording a number of sayings from the cross, all of which are positive. The first is the forgiveness saying, 'Father, forgive them; for they do not know what they are doing' (23:34). The second is the promise to the penitent thief that 'today you will be with me in Paradise' (23:43). And the third, Jesus' final words from the cross, is 'Father, into your hands I commend my spirit' (23:46). As can be seen overleaf, Matthew and Mark are almost identical but Luke and John are significantly different.

Now up to this point, the Church had accepted the judgement of Augustine that Matthew was the first Gospel to be written and that Mark was an abbreviation of it (it is about two-thirds the length). But during the nineteenth century, scholars became more and more convinced that Mark was the first Gospel and that both Matthew and

Matthew 7:45–46	Mark 15:33–34	Luke 23:44–46	John 19:28–30
From noon on, darkness came over the whole land until three in the afternoon. And about three o'clock Jesus cried with a loud voice, 'Eli, Eli, lema sabachthani?' that is, 'My God, my God, why have you forsaken me?'	When it was noon, darkness came over the whole land until three in the afternoon. At three o'clock Jesus cried out with a loud voice, 'Eloi, Eloi, lema sabachthani?' which means, 'My God, my God, why have you forsaken me?'	It was now about noon, and darkness came over the whole land until three in the afternoon, while the sun's light failed; and the curtain of the temple was torn in two. Then Jesus, crying with a loud voice, said, 'Father, into your hands I commend my spirit.' Having said this, he breathed his last.	After this, when Jesus knew that all was now finished, he said (in order to fulfill the scripture), 'I am thirsty.' A jar full of sour wine was standing there. So they put a sponge full of the wine on a branch of hyssop and held it to his mouth. When Jesus had received the wine, he said, 'It is finished.' Then he bowed his head and gave up his spirit.

Luke used Mark as one of their sources. If this is true, then historical reconstruction suggests that the original picture of Jesus dying in despair (or at least questioning God) was changed to a more victorious one. It is true that Matthew follows Mark by repeating the cry of dereliction but he offsets this by telling us that when Jesus died, there was an earthquake, the tombs opened and the saints of old came to life (Matt 27:51–53). Though the cry of despair is recorded, the reader is left in no doubt that Jesus' death was a victory. It was nothing short of the beginning of the resurrection of the dead (Ezek 37:13: 'And you shall know that I am the Lord, when I open your graves, and bring you up from your graves, O my people').

Luke's changes are more far-reaching. He omits the cry altogether and replaces it with 'Father, into your hands I commend my spirit' (a quotation from Ps 31:5). The other two sayings have already indicated that Jesus is thinking of others rather than himself. Now he indicates his complete submission to God. He willingly commends his spirit into God's hands. There is no sense of despair or questioning God. As Talbert (*Reading Luke*, 1982) says, 'Jesus dies quietly, full of trust, a model for Christian martyrs to follow'.[5] His promise to the penitent thief ('today you will be with me in Paradise') is also a sign of his own confidence. This day he will be in paradise.

John is even further away from Mark. He is similar to Luke in having Jesus thinking of others (his mother) instead of his own suffering. But is this quite accurate? One looks in vain in John's account to find any suggestion that Jesus is really suffering. He asks for a drink, which he duly takes. But this was to fulfil Scripture, not because he was in need. And then he utters his final words, 'It is finished'. Jesus has come from the Father, has accomplished his will and now returns. Our knowledge of the other Gospels (and the creeds) tells us that Jesus suffered but it is not John's focus. The impression left by the Gospel of John is more that Jesus, as divine Son of God, rose above the pain and died victoriously. Everything had gone as planned.

Some try to minimize the differences between these accounts by suggesting that the so-called cry of dereliction is really a cry of victory. As is well known, the cry is a quotation from the beginning of Psalm 22 ('My God, my God, why have you forsaken me? Why are you so far from helping me, from the words of my groaning?'). However, the psalm does end on a note of trust:

> To him, indeed, shall all who sleep in the earth bow down; before him shall bow all who go down to the dust, and I shall live for him. Posterity will serve him; future generations will be told about the Lord, and proclaim his deliverance to a people yet unborn, saying that he has done it. (22:29–31)

However, it would be a strange way of pointing to the 'trusting' part of the psalm by quoting only from the 'despairing' part. One could perhaps argue that Jesus was intending to recite the whole of the psalm but got no further than the first line. But that hardly lends itself to harmonizing with John or Luke, where the last words are positive and affirming. The most natural way of reading Mark's crucifixion account is that Jesus died in turmoil if not despair. And the words of Psalm 22:1 were on his lips because they voiced what he was feeling. He identified with the (innocent) suffering of the psalmist.

Furthermore, such differences between the Gospels are not limited to the crucifixion scene. Consider, for example, how each of the Gospels begins. Mark has Jesus coming to John for baptism (1:9), receiving the Holy Spirit (1:10) and hearing a heavenly voice (1:11). If we did not possess the other Gospels, there would be no reason to assume that Jesus was anything special before this experience. He was simply one of the many who came to John for baptism. In Mark's account, what sets Jesus apart is what happened to him *at* his baptism. The heavens opened, the Spirit descended, the voice spoke. This is what empowered him to do battle with Satan (1:12–13) and begin a ministry of preaching, healing and exorcism. In terms of later doctrinal disputes, Mark could be open to an 'adoptionist' view of Christ, the view that God chose Jesus to be the Messiah and hence 'Son of God'.

Matthew and Luke, by providing infancy stories, rule out this interpretation. Jesus was no ordinary man who simply received the Spirit at baptism. The Spirit was involved in his life from the very moment of conception (indeed, conception was of the Holy Spirit). It is probable that this is more important to the authors than the so-called virgin birth, which is never referred to again in the whole of the New Testament (see R. E. Brown, *The Birth of the Messiah*, 1977). But now that we know that Jesus is set apart at birth and endowed with the Spirit, we are ready for a different sort of baptism account. And that is what Matthew offers:

> Then Jesus came from Galilee to John at the Jordan, to be baptized by him. John would have prevented him, saying, 'I need to be baptized by you, and do you come to me?' But Jesus answered him, 'Let it be so now; for it is proper for us in this way to fulfill all righteousness.' (3:13–15)

Matthew and Luke rule out the possibility that Jesus was simply adopted by God at his baptism. God's Spirit was involved from the very moment of conception, and the incident of the boy Jesus in the temple (Luke 2:41–51) and the baptism story in Matthew confirm this. However, in neither Gospel is there any hint that Jesus had a 'life' with God before his conception. The virgin birth might be miraculous but it is nevertheless narrating the beginning or origin of Jesus' life. There is no suggestion in Matthew or Luke that Jesus' birth is the incarnation of a pre-existent being. But that is precisely what John claims in the opening of his Gospel:

> In the beginning was the Word, and the Word was with God, and the Word was God. He was in the beginning with God. All things came into being through him, and without him not one thing came into being... And the Word became flesh and lived among us, and we have seen his glory, the glory as of a father's only son, full of grace and truth. (1:1–3, 14)

The quest for the historical Jesus

Whatever the processes that led to the sort of differences that we have been highlighting, the Church has generally assumed them to be providential. It is admitted that John's Gospel has a much more explicit Christology (doctrine of Christ) than Mark but this is part of an unfolding revelation which eventually led to the definition of Chalcedon (451 CE) and the creeds:

Therefore, following the holy Fathers, we all with one accord teach men to acknowledge one and the same Son, our Lord Jesus Christ, at once complete in Godhead and complete in manhood, truly God and truly man, consisting also of a reasonable soul and body; of one substance with the Father as regards his Godhead, and at the same time of one substance with us as regards his manhood; like us in all respects, apart from sin; as regards his Godhead, begotten of the Father before the ages, but yet as regards his manhood begotten, for us men and for our salvation, of Mary the Virgin, the God-bearer; one and the same Christ, Son, Lord, Only-begotten, recognized in two natures, without confusion, without change, without division, without separation; the distinction of natures being in no way annulled by the union, but rather the characteristics of each nature being preserved and coming together to form one person and subsistence, not as parted or separated into two persons, but one and the same Son and Only-begotten God the Word, Lord Jesus Christ; even as the prophets from earliest times spoke of him, and our Lord Jesus Christ himself taught us, and the creed of the Fathers has handed down to us.[6]

However, if history means anything, it is difficult to maintain that this complex set of propositions was what 'our Lord Jesus Christ himself taught us'. It may represent genuine hindsight as to his significance but it is a long way from our earliest source (Mark). The Jesus of Mark is more concerned to preach the kingdom of God than instruct his disciples that he is 'of one substance with the Father as regards his Godhead, and at the same time of one substance with us as regards his manhood'. So what sort of picture of Jesus emerges if we allow Mark to be our guide? For Albert Schweitzer (*The Quest of the Historical Jesus*, 1910), it was of someone who ardently believed that the end of the world was near:

Now after John was arrested, Jesus came to Galilee, proclaiming the good news of God, and saying, 'The time is fulfilled, and the kingdom of God has come near; repent, and believe in the good news.' (Mark 1:14–15)

Truly I tell you, there are some standing here who will not taste death until they see that the kingdom of God has come with power. (Mark 9:1)

Truly I tell you, this generation will not pass away until all these things have taken place. (Mark 13:30)

Jesus' mission, says Schweitzer, was to prepare Israel for the coming kingdom of God. Jesus initially thought this would come as a result of his ministry (Matt 10:23) but when this did not happen, he went to

Jerusalem to bring it about. It resulted in his death. The end did not come; it still has not come and Christians must face up to the fact that Jesus was therefore mistaken. And the cry of dereliction reflects this. Jesus could not understand why God had not intervened and ushered in the kingdom. His final words indicate both his disappointment and his perplexity: 'My God, my God, *why* have you forsaken me?' After centuries of cover-up, Schweitzer urged Christians to face up to the facts about Jesus. He was not the doctrinal figure of the creeds, fully aware of his own divinity and knowing everything in advance. Indeed, Jesus states this quite clearly in Mark 13:32: 'But about that day or hour no one knows, neither the angels in heaven, nor the Son, but only the Father.'

So who was Jesus? For Schweitzer, he was an eschatological prophet, a preacher of the end of the world (*eschatos* = end). This is the reason for his radical teaching on discipleship. The end is coming soon and so no sacrifice is too great in order to be ready. Possessions and family must not be allowed to get in the way (Mark 10:28–31). Let the dead bury their own dead (Matt 9:22). If hand or foot causes you to stumble, cut it off (Mark 9:43). Such radical commands make sense in a time of crisis or dire emergency but are hardly a blueprint for a healthy society (especially if taken literally). And if we are honest, we must recognize that we would normally associate such behaviour (broken families, harsh treatment of the body) with fanatical sects, rather than Christianity.

Schweitzer's views did not go unchallenged. C. H. Dodd (*The Parables of the Kingdom*, 1935) pointed out that there are other sayings in the Gospels which suggest that Jesus believed the kingdom to have actually arrived. Thus, in the Beelzebub controversy (Mark 3:22–30), Jesus implies that his healings and exorcisms are a result of God's kingdom attacking Satan's kingdom. This is made more explicit in Matthew's version, which says: 'But if it is by the Spirit of God that I cast out demons, then the kingdom of God has come to you' (12:28). Dodd believed that the urgency in Jesus' ministry was not because the kingdom was coming soon but because it was already making its presence felt. Jesus himself is the event that forces people to decide for or against the kingdom, not the end of the world. God was 'realizing' or 'making present' his kingdom in Jesus and hence the urgency of his message.

Dodd's view was later to be called 'realized' eschatology as opposed to Schweitzer's 'futurist' eschatology. But what of the three verses in Mark (1:15; 9:1; 13:30) that seem to imply that the end of the world is coming soon? Dodd offered alternative interpretations. For Mark 1:15, the phrase 'the kingdom of God has come near' means it has actually arrived. The announcement is not saying that the kingdom is coming soon; anyone could have said that. The point is that, in Jesus, the future hope has actually been realized. And Dodd supported this interpretation by pointing out that the Greek verb (*engizein* = to draw near) is in the perfect tense and therefore implies a completed state. In other words, the kingdom has drawn near to such an extent that it has actually arrived in the person of Jesus.

On Mark 9:1, he says: 'The bystanders are not promised that they shall see the Kingdom of God *coming*, but that they shall come to see that the Kingdom of God *has already come*, at some point before they became aware of it.'[7] Once again, he points out that the verb 'coming' (a participle) is in the perfect tense and should be translated 'has already come'. And thirdly, the calamities to take place in the disciples' generation (Mark 13:30) refer to the political upheavals mentioned in the first part of the discourse (13:5–23), not the end of the world. And if these calamities refer to the Jewish war (*c.* 66–70 CE), as Luke makes explicit with his mention of 'Jerusalem surrounded by armies' (Luke 21:20), then they did indeed take place within a generation.

Dodd's linguistic arguments are now regarded as dubious but his work was an important corrective to Schweitzer. The consensus for the last forty years has been that the kingdom of God is both present and future. There are sayings that suggest that Jesus believed the kingdom to be present in his own ministry. But, equally, there are sayings which suggest a future dimension and this is usually referred to as 'the consummation'. The kingdom was inaugurated by Jesus but awaits a final consummation. Nevertheless, the impression given by Mark is undoubtedly that the consummation was expected soon, a view shared by Paul:

> For the Lord himself, with a cry of command, with the archangel's call and with the sound of God's trumpet, will descend from heaven, and the dead in Christ will rise first. *Then we who are alive, who are left*, will be caught up in the clouds together with them to meet the Lord in the air; and so we will be with the Lord forever. (1 Thess 4:16–17)

> I mean, brothers and sisters, the appointed time has grown short; from now on, let even those who have wives be as though they had none, and those who mourn as though they were not mourning, and those who rejoice as though they were not rejoicing, and those who buy as though they had no possessions, and those who deal with the world as though they had no dealings with it. *For the present form of this world is passing away*. (1 Cor 7:29–31)

The Jesus Seminar

In 1985, under the leadership of Robert Funk, around 70 to 100 North American scholars agreed to meet twice a year to study all the recorded sayings of Jesus. Their purpose, says Funk, was 'to examine every fragment of the traditions attached to the name of Jesus in order to determine what he really said – not his literal words, perhaps, but the substance and style of his utterances'.[8] Each seminar took as its theme a particular aspect of the sayings tradition (e.g. parables, aphorisms, Sermon on the Mount) and after papers were discussed and opinions shared, a vote was taken. Each scholar was asked to cast a vote depending on whether they thought a particular saying was definitely from Jesus (red), probably from Jesus (pink), probably not from Jesus (grey) and definitely not from Jesus (black). The results have now been published in *The Five Gospels: The Search for the Authentic Words of Jesus* (1993).

It came as no surprise that almost the whole of John's Gospel is in black. For the last two centuries, the Fourth Gospel has been regarded as a sublime theological reflection rather than recording the actual words of Jesus (though John Robinson's *The Priority of John*, 1985, suggests this has been overdone). But what was a surprise is that the Seminar turned its back on the eschatological consensus of Schweitzer and Dodd (and its modern exponents, such as E. P. Sanders) in favour of a non-eschatological Jesus. Rather than seeing 1 Thessalonians 4:16–17 and 1 Corinthians 7:29–31 as continuing Jesus' eschatological hope, the Seminar thought such fervour belonged to the early Church and was generated by Jesus' resurrection. Writing in the midst of the Jewish war (*c.* 66–70 CE), it is Mark who believes the end is nigh, not Jesus:

> The evidence of his parables and aphorisms shows that Jesus did not understand the rule of God to be the beginning of a new age, at the end of history, following a cosmic catastrophe. And he certainly did not speak of God's domain in the nationalistic sense of a revival of David's kingdom. Rather, in the judgment of the Seminar, Jesus spoke most characteristically of God's rule as close or already present but unrecognized, and thus in a way that challenged both apocalyptic and nationalistic expectations.[9]

Conclusion

For most of church history, the meaning of the Bible was whatever the hierarchy of the Church decided. And, as Galileo found out, it had means of persuasion for those who disagreed. But the Enlightenment changed that by suggesting that truth should be established by rational enquiry, not 'law and enforcement'. Central to this was the use of the historical method. By evaluating sources and suggesting hypotheses, here was a means of enquiry with which all could agree. Any rational person must concede that Moses could not have written every word of the Pentateuch and Jesus did not go around talking about his two natures. The evidence says so.

However, debate continued as to the significance of this evidence. Radical scholars saw it as the tip of the iceberg. If editors were still working on the Pentateuch in the fifth century BCE, then it is hardly a reliable source for what Moses said and did a thousand years earlier. The Pentateuch, as we now have it, represents what Israelite tradition *believed* about Moses, not what he actually said and did. On the other hand, conservative scholars pointed out that the number of verses that definitely could not have been written by Moses is relatively small. The different styles could represent the sources used by Moses or even changes in his own style over a period of forty years or more. It is therefore still possible to view the Pentateuch as *substantially* the work of Moses, even though later editors have added explanatory remarks ('before any king reigned over the Israelites').

Furthermore, it was argued that the Bible can only be regarded as mistaken if it can be shown (for example) that the author of Genesis intended the 'six days' to be taken literally or that Jesus intended to predict the date of his second coming. In the first case, it has long been observed that the sun was not created until the fourth day (Gen 1:14–19) and so 'days' does not necessarily imply twenty-four-hour periods (which are governed by the sun). And Mark 13:32 makes it clear that Jesus refused to speculate about when the end would come. In other words, the truth of a passage depends on what the author or speaker was intending. If the Gospel writers were aiming to give us the exact words of Jesus, then the fact that they differ must mean that one or more of them is in error. But was that their intention?

FURTHER READING

A useful summary of Pentateuchal criticism and the relationship between the Gospels can be found in chs 1 and 40 of the *New Jerome Biblical Commentary*. For a more detailed examination of the Pentateuch, see R. N. Whybray, *The Making of the Pentateuch* (Sheffield Academic Press, 1987). And for detailed study of the relationship between the Synoptic Gospels, see *Studying the Synoptic Gospels* by E. P. Sanders and M. Davies (SCM/Trinity Press, 1989). This large-size book is set out like a workbook, with diagrams, charts and Gospel parallels and also includes chapters on Form and Redaction Criticism, Literary approaches and 'Life of Jesus' research. Highly recommended.

NOTES

1. Quoted in C. H. Dodd, *The Parables of the Kingdom* (Fount edition, 1978), p. 13.
2. E. J. Young, *An Introduction to the Old Testament* (Eerdmans, 1964), p. 45.
3. S. R. Driver, *The Book of Genesis* (Westminster Commentaries; Methuen, 1904), p. 321.
4. *An Introduction to the Old Testament*, p. 153.
5. C. H. Talbert, *Reading Luke* (SPCK, 1982), p. 225.
6. Taken from H. Bettenson (ed.), *Documents of the Christian Church* (2nd edn; Oxford University Press, 1963), pp. 51–2 (omitting Greek).
7. *Parables of the Kingdom*, p. 43, n. 28.
8. Quoted in M. Borg, *Jesus in Contemporary Scholarship* (Trinity Press International, 1994), p. 161.
9. Robert W. Funk, Roy W. Hoover, and the Jesus Seminar, *The Five Gospels: The Search for the Authentic Words of Jesus* (Polebridge Press, 1993), p. 40.

3

The Bible and its human authors

In 1919, Karl Ludwig Schmidt published a book (*Der Rahmen der Geschichte Jesu*) which showed that many of the events in the Gospels are introduced with a minimum of historical detail. For example, the story of the disciples passing through the grainfields is introduced by the words 'One sabbath he was going through the grainfields' (Mark 2:23). It is important for the story that it happened on a sabbath but, other than that, there is no indication whether this happened early in the ministry or much later. Mark's next story begins 'Again he entered the synagogue' (3:1), which only tells us that this was not his first visit. It could come from any time in Jesus' ministry. We assume it is early because it comes early in Mark's Gospel. But is that a safe assumption? Matthew obviously did not think Mark's order was sacrosanct, as can be seen from the following comparison. Notice, in particular, the positions of the 'stilling of the storm' (12) and the interwoven stories of Jairus, the woman with the issue of blood and Jairus' daughter (14):

Mark	*Matthew*
1 Call of the fishermen	Call of the fishermen (1)
2 Exorcism in synagogue	Sermon on the Mount
3 Peter's mother-in-law	Healing of leper (4)
4 Healing of leper	Centurion's slave
5 Healing of paralytic	Peter's mother-in-law (3)
6 Call of Levi	Stilling of storm (12)
7 Grainfields	Gadarene demoniac (13)
8 Withered hand	Healing of paralytic (5)
9 Appointing of the twelve	Call of Levi (6)
10 Beelzebub controversy	Jairus/Woman with issue of
11 Parables of sower/lamp/seed	blood/Jairus' daughter (14)
12 Stilling of storm	Healing of two blind men
13 Gerasene demoniac	Healing of a demoniac
14 Jairus/Woman with issue of	Appointing of the twelve (9)
blood/Jairus' daughter	Sending out of the twelve

The result of such observations led to *Formgeschichte* (form history) or, in English, form criticism. Schmidt argued that the various stories about Jesus were transmitted separately (in sermons, catechism, debate with the Jews) and it is the Gospel writers who are responsible for the framework. For the following half-century, scholars such as Martin Dibelius (1919) and Rudolf Bultmann (1921)[1] tried to determine how such traditions were modified during transmission. For example, were the miracle stories abbreviated (to focus on the point) or expanded (to make them more astounding)? Were the passion predictions (Mark 8:31; 9:31; 10:33) made more specific by the addition of 'and after three days rise again'? And are the allegorical elements in the parables original (Mark 4:14–20), or the work of the early Church?

Bultmann's conclusions were radical. What we now have in the Gospels is a long way from what was actually said and done. General statements, such as the appropriateness of rejoicing at a wedding (Mark 2:19), have become predictions of the crucifixion ('The days will come when the bridegroom is taken away from them'). The command to make disciples (Matt 28:19) now includes baptism in the name of Father, Son and Holy Spirit (completely absent from Acts). On the other hand, scholars such as Gerhardsson (*Memory and Manuscript*, 1961) argued that, at the time of Christ, Jewish traditions were not treated like folk stories. Some Rabbis knew the whole of the Pentateuch (Torah) off by heart. By rote learning and memory techniques, Gerhardsson believed that Jewish tradition was handed down from generation to generation, almost without error. And since Mark's Gospel was written within a single generation of the death of Jesus, there is little reason to doubt its basic authenticity.

However, in the 1960s, attention turned away from sources and traditions (always hypothetical) to the authors themselves. If it is true that Matthew and Luke both used Mark as one of their sources, then we can actually see what changes they were prepared to make. The result was the birth of *Redaktionsgeschichte*. Redaction criticism, as it is known in English, seeks to determine the outlook and purpose of the author. By analysing changes of wording, order and emphasis, redaction criticism aims to give a rationale for why the authors wrote as they did. It operates on the belief that such changes are not arbitrary but are clues to the intention of the author. What source and form criticism regarded as secondary ('the cement'), redaction criticism regards as primary – for it reveals the mind of the author.

Luke's changes to Mark

We have already mentioned that Luke adds two chapters of infancy stories to Mark's opening. One effect of this is to show that Jesus was not simply a penitent coming for baptism but that his birth (and conception) was of the Holy Spirit. Another characteristic is that they centre on Jerusalem. Zechariah and Elizabeth were 'righteous before God' (Luke 1:6) and it was while Zechariah was performing his priestly duties that the birth of John the Baptist was announced. Incidentally, one would never have guessed from Mark that John and Jesus were cousins. Indeed, it might have been part of Luke's purpose to clarify the relationship between John and Jesus, since Acts 19:1–7 makes it clear that not all of John's disciples became followers of Jesus.

At the end of the Gospel, Luke makes changes to the crucifixion scene, as we have already noted. The effect is to present a much more assured picture of Jesus, a martyr who dies asking for the forgiveness of his enemies. Luke also adds a number of resurrection appearances, the most memorable being the walk to Emmaus. It is surely a significant aspect of this story that the disciples recognize Jesus when he breaks bread (Luke 24:30–31), just as, in Acts, the early Christians will meet to break bread (Acts 2:46). The majority of scholars believe that the Gospel of Luke and the Acts of the Apostles were written by the same person (they are both addressed to a certain Theophilus: Luke 1:3; Acts 1:1).

However, Luke's biggest change in terms of quantity of material is his so-called 'travel narrative'. According to Mark, after the transfiguration (Mark 9:2–13) and healing of the epileptic boy (Mark 9:14–32), Jesus returns to Capernaum and utters sayings about 'first and last', 'causing people to stumble' and acting as salt (Mark 9:33–50). Then, in Mark 10:1, he sets off for Judaea, has a discussion with the Pharisees about divorce (Mark 10:2–12) and blesses the children (10:13–16). The corresponding sequence in Luke is as follows:

Mark	*Luke*
Transfiguration	Transfiguration
Epileptic boy	Epileptic boy
Various sayings	Various sayings
Begins journey	Begins journey
	Mission and return of the seventy
	Parable of the Good Samaritan
	Mary and Martha
	Lord's Prayer
	Beelzebub controversy
	Woes against Pharisees and scribes
	Parable of the rich fool
	The faithful steward
	Parable of the fig tree
	The woman with the eighteen-year infirmity

(cont.)

Mark	Luke
	Parables of the mustard seed and leaven
	Lament over Jerusalem
	Healing of the man with dropsy
	Parable of the wedding banquet
	Parables of the lost coin, sheep, son
	Parable of the unrighteous steward
	Parable of the rich man and Lazarus
	Healing of ten lepers
	The coming of the Son of man
	Parable of the unrighteous judge
	Parable of the Pharisee and the publican
Question of divorce	
Blessing of the children	Blessing of the children
Rich young ruler	Rich young ruler

This extra material is rich in parables and wisdom sayings, and Hans Conzelmann (1953) believed that Luke was consciously altering Mark's picture of Jesus. Whether Jesus looked for the actual arrival of the kingdom or its consummation, the picture of Jesus in Mark remains an eschatological one. However, Christians at the end of the first century had to face up to the fact that Jesus had not returned. Far from seeing the kingdom coming in their lifetime, they had seen most of the disciples die. That this was a problem for the early Church can be seen from the following:

> Peter turned and saw the disciple whom Jesus loved following them; he was the one who had reclined next to Jesus at the supper and had said, 'Lord, who is it that is going to betray you?' When Peter saw him, he said to Jesus, 'Lord, what about him?' Jesus said to him, 'If it is my will that he remain until I come, what is that to you? Follow me!' So the rumour spread in the community that this disciple would not die. Yet Jesus did not say to him that he would not die, but, 'If it is my will that he remain until I come, what is that to you?' (John 21:20–23)

> First of all you must understand this, that in the last days scoffers will come... saying, 'Where is the promise of his coming? For ever since our ancestors died, all things continue as they were from the beginning of creation!'... But do not ignore this one fact, beloved, that with the Lord one day is like a thousand years, and a thousand years are like one day. The Lord is not slow about his promise, as some think of slowness, but is patient with you, not wanting any to perish, but all to come to repentance. But the day of the Lord will come like a thief, and then the heavens will pass away with a loud noise, and the elements will be dissolved with fire... (2 Pet 3:3–10)

Conzelmann argued that Luke dealt with the issue by dividing history into three periods. The first period is that of the Old Testament, a period of anticipation and prediction. He made the point that whereas Mark portrays John the Baptist as the forerunner of the new age, Luke makes him the last of the old age (Luke 16:16). Second, there is the period of Christ's earthly ministry, where the devil is bound and his kingdom plundered. This is the subject of Luke's first volume and why the original German title of Conzelmann's work was *Die Mitte der Zeit* ('The Middle of Time').[2] Third, there is an indefinite period until the Lord returns. This is the church age and the subject of Luke's second volume. It is traditionally called 'The Acts of the Apostles' but a better title might be 'The Continuing Acts of Jesus through his Church'. This schematizing of history allowed Christians of the late first century to understand their role positively rather than lamenting Jesus' failure to return.

If this is correct, then Luke's most difficult task was to do something with those three sayings in Mark which seem to stress the nearness of the end. He appears to have done so. Thus the first is reworded so as to eliminate any sense of an imminent end:

Now after John was arrested, Jesus came to Galilee, proclaiming the good news of God, and saying, 'The time is fulfilled, and the kingdom of God has come near; repent, and believe in the good news.' (Mark 1:14–15)	Then Jesus, filled with the power of the Spirit, returned to Galilee, and a report about him spread through all the surrounding country. He began to teach in their synagogues and was praised by everyone. (Luke 4:14–15)

The second (Mark 9:1 = Luke 9:27) is modified by omitting three words. The promise is no longer that the disciples will see the kingdom '*coming in power*' (seemingly pointing to the end of the world) but only that they will see the kingdom. Thus the disciples will live to see the kingdom but not necessarily its consummation ('*coming in power*'). This could therefore refer to the transfiguration, Jesus' resurrection, Pentecost or the fall of Jerusalem. There is no reason to take the saying as referring to the end of the world.

The third saying (Mark 13:30 = Luke 21:32) is the most difficult as it comes at the climax of what is often called the apocalyptic discourse (Mark 13), where sun and moon collapse and the 'Son of man' comes on the clouds. Luke reproduces most of this but introduces a clause in between the fall of Jerusalem and the coming of the 'Son of man'. Its effect is to suggest that an indefinite period (the church age) separates the destruction of Jerusalem (which Luke makes more explicit by mentioning armies) from the signs in sun and moon:

Mark 13:14–30	*Luke 21:20–32*
But when you see the desolating sacrilege set up where it ought not to be (let the reader understand), then those in Judea must flee to the mountains...	When you see Jerusalem surrounded by armies, then know that its desolation has come near. Then those in Judea must flee to the mountains...
	and Jerusalem will be trampled on by the Gentiles, until the times of the Gentiles are fulfilled.
But in those days, after that suffering, the sun will be darkened, and the moon will not give its light...	There will be signs in the sun, the moon, and the stars, and on the earth distress among nations...
Then they will see 'the Son of Man coming in clouds' with great power and glory...	Then they will see 'the Son of Man coming in a cloud' with power and great glory...
From the fig tree learn its lesson: as soon as its branch becomes tender and puts forth its leaves, you know that summer is near. So also, when you see these things taking place, you know that he is near, at the very gates.	Look at the fig tree and all the trees; as soon as they sprout leaves you can see for yourselves and know that summer is already near. So also, when you see these things taking place, you know that the kingdom of God is near.
Truly I tell you, this generation will not pass away until all these things have taken place.	Truly I tell you, this generation will not pass away until all things have taken place.

Some of Conzelmann's points are disputed but most scholars would agree that Luke has made significant changes to Mark. The extra material, along with specific changes of wording, do give the Gospel a different emphasis. As Norman Perrin (*What Is Redaction Criticism?*, 1970) observes, it is thanks to Conzelmann that scholars now see Luke as a major theologian rather than simply a collector of traditions. Even those that challenge Conzelmann write books with titles like *Luke: Historian and Theologian* (I. H. Marshall, 1989).

Matthew's changes to Mark

Like Luke, Matthew adds infancy stories (focusing on Joseph rather than Mary), resurrection accounts (in Galilee) and a great deal of teaching and parables. However, Matthew does not include this teaching material in one long travel narrative but constructs five great discourses, perhaps on the pattern of the five books of the Law. There is a discourse on righteousness (chs 5 – 7, usually called the Sermon on the Mount), on missionary work (ch. 10), on the kingdom (ch. 13), on the Church (ch. 18) and on things to come (chs 24 – 25). Two of these (the kingdom and the apocalyptic discourse) are expansions of Mark 4 and 13 respectively but the other three are down to Matthew, who seems to have had an eye for symmetry:

1	Genealogy and birth of Jesus
2	Magi and escape to Egypt
3	Baptism
4	Temptation, calling of disciples
5	**Righteousness Discourse**
6	**(Sermon on the Mount)**
7	
8	Healing of leper and centurion
9	Healing of paralytic
10	**Missionary Discourse**
11	Jesus and John the Baptist
12	Jesus and Beelzebub
13	**Kingdom Discourse**
14	Feeding of 5,000
15	Feeding of 4,000
16	Peter's confession
17	Transfiguration
18	**Church Discourse**
19	Journey to Jerusalem
20	Parable of workers in vineyard
21	Triumphal entry
22	Parable of wedding banquet
23	Woes against Pharisees
24	**Apocalyptic Discourse**
25	
26	Last supper, Gethsemane
27	Crucifixion
28	Resurrection appearances

Explanations for these changes vary but most agree that it is something to do with Matthew providing the Church with a pattern of teaching. Mark tells us that Jesus taught with great authority (Mark

1:27) but does not actually reproduce much of his teaching. Matthew offers guidance to the Church in the areas of moral decisions, missionary strategy and church discipline. Further, the discourses on the kingdom and eschatology go some way to answering the question of what Christians should be doing while they wait for Jesus' return. This emphasis on the Church can be seen by the fact that Matthew is the only Gospel to use the Greek word *ekklēsia*:

> And I tell you, you are Peter, and on this rock I will build my church (*ekklēsia*), and the gates of Hades will not prevail against it. (16:18)

> If the member refuses to listen to them, tell it to the church (*ekklēsia*); and if the offender refuses to listen even to the church (*ekklēsia*), let such a one be to you as a Gentile and a tax collector. (18:17)

If these sayings go back to Jesus, he probably used a general Aramaic word meaning 'gathering' or 'congregation'. By using the Greek word *ekklēsia*, Matthew has Jesus speak directly to the Church. Thus the Gospel is not simply a transparent record of what Jesus said and did but is shaped by the needs of the Church. Matthew emphasizes those things that he thinks his particular church needs to hear. Thus Robert Gundry entitles his commentary *Matthew: A Commentary on His Handbook for a Mixed Church under Persecution* (1994).

The Q hypothesis

So far, I may have given the impression that in order to change the emphasis of Mark, Matthew and Luke simply invented material. However, if this extra material in Matthew and Luke is analysed, it is found that some two hundred or so sayings are almost identical. For example, Mark has a very brief account of Jesus' temptation. This is expanded by both Matthew and Luke to include the three specific temptations of turning stones to bread, throwing himself off the temple and accepting the devil's offer of the kingdoms. Further, both omit Mark's mention of the wild animals and the angels ministering to Jesus. This would be an amazing coincidence if Matthew and Luke had acted independently:

Mark 1:12–13	*Matthew 4:1–4*	*Luke 4:1–4*
And the Spirit immediately drove him out into the wilderness. He was in the wilderness forty days, tempted by Satan;	Then Jesus was led up by the Spirit into the wilderness to be tempted by the devil. He fasted forty days and forty	Jesus, full of the Holy Spirit, returned from the Jordan and was led by the Spirit in the wilderness, where for

(cont.)

Mark 1:12–13	Matthew 4:1–4	Luke 4:1–4
and he was with the wild beasts; and the angels waited on him.	nights, and afterwards he was famished.	forty days he was tempted by the devil. He ate nothing at all during those days, and when they were over, he was famished.
	The tempter came and said to him, 'If you are the Son of God, command these stones to become loaves of bread.' But he answered, 'It is written, "One does not live by bread alone…" '	The devil said to him, 'If you are the Son of God, command this stone to become a loaf of bread.' Jesus answered him, 'It is written, "One does not live by bread alone." '

Even more revealing are the changes made to the preaching of John the Baptist. Here both Matthew and Luke complete Mark's sentence by adding the words 'and fire' and then go on to speak about the wheat and the chaff:

Mark 1:7–8	Matthew 3:11–12	Luke 3:16–17
'The one who is more powerful than I is coming after me; I am not worthy to stoop down and untie the thong of his sandals. I have baptized you with water; but he will baptize you with the Holy Spirit.'	'I baptize you with water for repentance, but one who is more powerful than I is coming after me; I am not worthy to carry his sandals.	'I baptize you with water; but one who is more powerful than I is coming; I am not worthy to untie the thong of his sandals.
	He will baptize you with the Holy Spirit and fire. His winnowing fork is in his hand, and he will clear his threshing floor and will gather his wheat into the granary; but the chaff he will burn with unquenchable fire.'	He will baptize you with the Holy Spirit and fire. His winnowing fork is in his hand, to clear his threshing floor and to gather the wheat into his granary; but the chaff he will burn with unquenchable fire.'

Some scholars, such as Michael Goulder (*Luke: A New Paradigm*, 1989), believe these similarities are best explained on the hypothesis that Luke had access to both Matthew and Mark. On this theory, Luke can see what Matthew has done with Mark and decide whether to follow him or not. Thus, in the example above, Luke begins with Matthew's 'I baptize you with water' but abbreviates by omitting 'for repentance' and 'after me'. He then changes to Mark, preferring 'untie the thong of his sandals' to Matthew's 'carry his sandals'. In English, the next phrase ('he will baptize you with the Holy Spirit') is the same in all three versions but, in the Greek, Luke agrees with Matthew (Mark omits the preposition *en*). He then continues by following Matthew's major addition to Mark, namely, the 'wheat and chaff' material, where there is close verbal agreement. Thus, providing we accept that Luke had access to Matthew (and many scholars do), Goulder offers a plausible explanation for the similarities and differences between the various versions.

However, many scholars find it difficult to believe that Matthew expanded Mark to form his five great teaching blocks, only to have Luke come along and obliterate them. If Luke is oscillating between Matthew and Mark, why does he take material away from its Markan setting in order to construct his long travel narrative? B. H. Streeter's view (*The Four Gospels: A Study of Origins*, 1924) was that Matthew and Luke both had access to a collection of sayings (conventionally called Q), which they drew on independently. Matthew used them to construct his five teaching blocks, while Luke used them to construct his long travel narrative. This would explain why there is often close verbal agreement in the individual sayings though they appear in very different settings.

Since Streeter's work, a great amount of effort has been expended in trying to reconstruct Q (see J. S. Kloppenborg, *The Formation of Q: Trajectories in Ancient Wisdom Collections*, 1987). For example, in the temptation narrative, Matthew speaks of turning 'stones to loaves' but Luke uses the singular. Which of these is closest to what was in Q? Further, the order of the temptations in Matthew is 'bread, temple, kingdoms' while in Luke, it is 'bread, kingdoms, temple'. What was the order in Q and why did either Matthew or Luke (or both) change it? The aim of such study was to illuminate the redactional work of Matthew and Luke.

More recently, however, the Q hypothesis has been taken up by the Jesus Seminar (along with the *Gospel of Thomas*) as a major source in the quest for the historical Jesus. Streeter realized that Q must have had alternative versions to some of Mark's stories. For example, John the Baptist could hardly have begun the 'wheat and chaff' saying with the words 'and fire'. At the very least, Q must have included the first part of the saying and some sort of introduction. In other words, Mark is not necessarily the earliest source for our knowledge of John the Baptist. Q offers a parallel version, which most scholars (who accept Q) regard as

earlier than Mark. What if the eschatological urgency found in Mark
(1:15; 9:1; 13:30) is due to Mark's particular circumstances (Nero's
persecution or the Jewish war), which Luke then corrects by drawing
on Q?

Q has played an important role in the individual reconstructions of
members of the Jesus Seminar. For example, it is key to Burton Mack's
A Myth of Innocence: Mark and Christian Origins (1988) and Dominic
Crossan's *The Historical Jesus: The Life of a Mediterranean Jewish
Peasant* (1991). Neither of these is an easy read and those new to the
subject will profit from first reading Marcus Borg's *Jesus in
Contemporary Scholarship* (1994). Borg's own view is that Jesus was
primarily a wisdom teacher and holy man, challenging the power
structures (Roman and Jewish) of his day. Jesus did this not by
offering a blueprint for change (the liberal portrait), nor by threatening
people with the end of the world (the eschatological portrait). Rather,
'Jesus spoke of a very different vision of life. His message as a wisdom
teacher contained a twofold dynamic: subversion of the central
convictions of conventional wisdom and invitation to a path of
transformation that led to an alternative way of life.'[3] He continues:

> For most sages, the wise way was the way of conventional wisdom
> itself, and the foolish way was the path of disregarding conventional
> wisdom. Jesus reversed this: he spoke of the broad way which led to
> destruction, not as gross wickedness or flagrant foolishness, but as
> the way of conventional wisdom. He consistently undermined the
> focal points of his social world's conventional wisdom (wealth,
> honor, the patriarchal family, purity, religiosity), sometimes gently
> mocking and other times sharply ridiculing the concerns which
> animate and imprison people.[4]

Many would agree with this assessment without agreeing with Borg
that it is incompatible with an eschatological Jesus. Indeed, since both
John the Baptist and the early Church were firmly eschatological, it is
difficult to believe that Jesus had no interest in the future. It is also true
that Q itself is not devoid of eschatological sayings, which Borg and
other members of the Seminar regard as later additions. Nevertheless,
it may be that too much emphasis has been placed on a few 'end of
world' sayings to the detriment of the large body of wisdom traditions.

Mark and John

Though scholars analyse the data differently, the differences between
Matthew and Mark or Luke and Mark do provide something objective
with which to work. But what of the purposes of Mark and John? We

do not have access to their sources and so cannot tell what changes they made. To a limited degree, we can isolate editorial comment (Mark 13:14; John 2:21), summaries (Mark 1:34; John 20:30) and explanations (Mark 7:19; John 7:39), which are clues to their outlook and purpose. But by and large, the only way forward is to try and determine the main themes of the Gospel and assume that these are the things the author wished to emphasize. Some have called this 'composition criticism' but whether the main thrust of the Gospel is the result of the author's editing or came to him in his sources remains speculative.

It is clear from comparing Mark with the other Gospels that it particularly emphasizes the failure of the disciples. Incident after incident shows them in a bad light. Even after the feeding of the five thousand, they have no idea how Jesus might feed a similar crowd of four thousand (Luke omits the second feeding). They want the best places in heaven, want to forbid children coming to him, criticize a woman who wants to anoint him and, in his hour of greatest need, desert him. How is this to be explained? One suggestion is that this is what actually happened and Matthew and Luke have progressively softened it (compare the conclusions of the 'walking on the water' story in Mark 6:50–52 and Matt 14:27–33). Alternatively, Mark might be emphasizing their failure for particular reasons. For example, perhaps he wants to give a warning against complacency. If even those closest to Jesus failed, no one can afford to be complacent but all must remain watchful (Mark 13:35).

We have already noted the sombre nature of the crucifixion scene and how Mark seems to spurn any attempt to make it victorious. This continues with his description of the empty tomb, for, according to our earliest manuscripts (see Chapter 6), Mark does not include any resurrection appearances. Instead, the Gospel ends on a note of awe:

Mark 16:6–8	Matthew 28:5–9
But he said to them, 'Do not be alarmed; you are looking for Jesus of Nazareth, who was crucified. He has been raised; he is not here.	But the angel said to the women, 'Do not be afraid; I know that you are looking for Jesus who was crucified. He is not here; for he has been raised, as he said.
Look, there is the place they laid him. But go, tell his disciples and Peter that he is going ahead of you to Galilee; there you will see him, just as he told you.'	Come, see the place where he lay. Then go quickly and tell his disciples, "He has been raised from the dead, and indeed he is going ahead of you to Galilee; there you will see him." This is my message for you.'

(cont.)

Mark 16:6–8	*Matthew 28:5–9*
So they went out and fled from the tomb, for terror and amazement had seized them; and they said nothing to anyone, for they were afraid.	So they left the tomb quickly with fear and great joy, and ran to tell his disciples.
	Suddenly Jesus met them and said, 'Greetings!' And they came to him, took hold of his feet, and worshipped him.

Why this dark portrait? According to Dennis Nineham (*Saint Mark*, 1963), Mark is writing to a persecuted church and highlights three things:

(a) That Jesus himself had suffered exactly as his followers were now being called upon to do.

(b) That Jesus had clearly warned his disciples that following him would involve sharing in his sufferings.

(c) That he had promised great and sure rewards to those who endured such sufferings without loss of faith.[5]

It is clear that Mark contains both 'suffering' passages (the cry of dereliction) and 'glory' passages (people were astounded by his miraculous power). Robert Gundry (*Mark: A Commentary on His Apology for the Cross*, 1993) thinks that Mark wishes to show that the crucified Jesus is none other than the all-powerful Lord. But most scholars think it is the other way around. Mark intends the 'glory' passages to be interpreted in the light of the 'suffering' passages. There can be no Christianity without the cross. Indeed, as Paul discovered, God's 'power is made perfect in weakness', rather than outward success (2 Cor 12:9). It is not that Mark does not believe in the resurrection. The empty tomb scene contains the promise: 'He has been raised; he is not here.' But he is not going to allow it to take away from the crucifixion. Nearly a third of Mark's Gospel (chs 11 – 16) focuses on the last week of his life (some have called Mark a 'passion narrative with a long introduction'). As Morna Hooker says:

> If we don't like Mark's ending, and think he cannot really have intended to end there, then perhaps it is because we are looking for the wrong thing. What we expect to find at the end of the Gospel is the knock-down proof, the evidence that proves that Jesus has indeed been raised from the dead, that he is the Messiah, the Son of God. But as with every other story in the Gospel, the evidence is there for those who have eyes to see it... For this is the real beginning of discipleship; and it is the beginning for Mark's own readers, who do not 'see' Jesus in any physical way.[6]

John's Gospel could not be more different. Not only does the author tell us that Jesus is the incarnation of the Word; Jesus is fully aware of it throughout the narrative. For example, in John 17:5, he is recorded as saying 'So now, Father, glorify me in your own presence with the glory that I had in your presence before the world existed'. How is this emphasis to be explained? One suggestion is that the Gospel emerged in a context of fierce disputes with the Jews. As Christians became more explicit about the divinity of Christ, so Jewish criticism became more vociferous. By the end of the century, the synagogue liturgy incorporated a curse on heretics, perhaps with the Christians in mind. The result was a Gospel that emphasized the following points:

(a) Jesus is fully divine. He is the incarnation of the Word and was recognized as such by any who had eyes to see. His death was his return to the Father.
(b) The Scriptures, when correctly interpreted, point to Jesus. The Jews do not see this because they are blind.
(c) Jesus specifically prophesied that Christians would be put out of the synagogue. The author of the Gospel even invents a Greek word for it. Christians will be made *asynagōgos* (de-synagogued).

Raymond Brown (*The Community of the Beloved Disciple*, 1979) takes this further by referring to the Johannine epistles. They are written in much the same style as the Gospel ('We declare to you what was from the beginning... the word of life... and declare to you the eternal life that was with the Father') but clearly have a different focus:

> By this you know the Spirit of God: every spirit that confesses that *Jesus Christ has come in the flesh* is from God, and every spirit that does not confess Jesus is not from God. (1 John 4:2)

> Many deceivers have gone out into the world, those who do not confess that *Jesus Christ has come in the flesh*; any such person is the deceiver and the antichrist! (2 John 7)

Brown points out that the target in the epistles is those who deny the humanity of Christ ('come in the flesh'). Now since John's Gospel placed a great deal of emphasis on the divinity of Christ, perhaps some took this too far and effectively denied his humanity. It is clear from 1 John 2:19 that there has been a split in the community ('They went out from us, but they did not belong to us; for if they had belonged to us, they would have remained with us. But by going out they made it plain that none of them belongs to us'). Brown believes this split concerns the proper interpretation of the Gospel. Some took its emphasis on divinity to mean that Jesus only 'seemed' to be human. After all, how can the divine Word need food or drink? When he appeared thirsty at the well (John 4:6–7), this is not to be taken literally. It was simply a device in order to engage the woman in conversation. And this is why there is no fear or pain at the crucifixion. Jesus is the Divine Word, who has taken the form of a man in order to communicate with us. But the reality is that Jesus is actually a divine being.

The epistles, however, insist that belief in the divinity of Christ must not be allowed to deny the fact that Jesus was a real human being. And the Gospel does portray Jesus as growing tired (4:6), feeling troubled (12:27), made of flesh and blood (19:34) and ultimately dying. If it is a paradox that a divine being can die, then the Gospel does not try to avoid it. Nevertheless, John's emphasis on the divinity of Christ (compare the arrest of Jesus in Mark 14:43–50 and John 18:1–11) is very different from the other three Gospels and requires some sort of explanation.

Summary

Redaction criticism suggests that what we have in the Gospels are four portraits of Jesus which were written to influence a particular group of readers. It is not denied that these accounts can be used to reconstruct his life but the results will always be open to debate. By focusing on the Evangelists, we appear to be on firmer ground. Thus we can say with a high degree of probability that Matthew sees Jesus as 'Teacher of the Church'. Whether this was actually a priority for Jesus (i.e. to prepare for an ongoing institution) will remain a matter for debate. But to have four attempts from the first century at applying the Jesus tradition to the needs of the Church is not to be despised. It speaks of a living faith, in continuity with the spirit of the first believers but not bound by the letter. Indeed, the fact that the Gospels are written in Greek shows that communication and relevance were more important to the Evangelists than preserving the actual words of Jesus (probably spoken in Aramaic).

Conservative scholars have naturally been concerned that redaction criticism has sometimes been used to challenge the historicity of the Gospels. They correctly point out that having a theological aim does not mean that the Evangelists had no interest in history. Thus Craig Blomberg (*The Historical Reliability of the Gospels*, 1987) describes redaction criticism in two paragraphs and then points out its weaknesses in ten. Nevertheless, he is able to conclude that 'when stripped of the excess baggage it tends to attract, it offers insights into the emphases of the evangelists which make the differences among the gospels understandable'.[7] And here is the key. Whatever one believes about inspiration, one cannot ignore the fact that the Gospels are very different. Indeed, the article in the IVP *Dictionary of Jesus and the Gospels* (1992) goes so far as to suggest that a proper understanding of inspiration *requires* a redactional understanding of the Gospels:

> A careful use of proper methodology can reduce the problems inherent in redaction criticism, and the values far outweigh the dangers. In fact, any study of the Gospels will be enhanced by redaction-critical techniques. A true understanding of the doctrine of inspiration demands it, for each Evangelist was led by God to utilize sources in the production of a Gospel. Moreover, they were given the freedom by God to omit, expand and highlight these traditions in order to bring out individual nuances peculiar to their own Gospel. Nothing else can explain the differing messages of the same stories as told in the various Gospels.[8]

Social-scientific criticism

One of the weaknesses of historical criticism is that it often focuses entirely on theological factors. Thus, if Paul's letters speak of dissension, it is assumed that there are various 'parties' who hold different doctrinal positions. But those of us who belong to a church community (or any club or society) know that most of the problems are not explicitly doctrinal but revolve around personalities, ways of doing things and traditions. We do not interact with one another as isolated 'theological minds' but through social structures. We are social beings and any attempt to explain why something happened must take this into account.

For example, in 1 Corinthians 8 – 10, Paul deals with the vexed question of whether Christians should eat meat which has previously been involved in pagan sacrifices. Some had no scruples, arguing that, since idols have no real existence, there is no question of the food becoming dangerous or contaminated. Indeed, it was a sign of their freedom in Christ to eat such food with a clear conscience (1 Cor 8:4–6). Others found it difficult, since for them it was equivalent to participating in the worship of idols, a view that Paul can also understand (1 Cor 10:14–22). Chapter 11 is also about food, the meal known as the Lord's supper. Paul castigates them for their behaviour: 'For when the time comes to eat, each of you goes ahead with your own supper, and one goes hungry and another becomes drunk. What! Do you not have homes to eat and drink in? Or do you show contempt for the church of God and humiliate those who have nothing?' (1 Cor

11:21–22). These have normally been explained as two quite separate issues, but is there a connection?

Prior to 1970, most commentaries focused on doctrinal explanations for these issues. What doctrine and beliefs were held by those that could eat the meat? What understanding of the sacraments underlies the divisions mentioned in chapter 11? But in a series of articles (now translated in *The Social Setting of Pauline Christianity*, 1982), Gerd Theissen asked whether certain social factors could help explain these passages. In one article ('Social stratification in the Corinthian community'), he notes that the church at Corinth contained both rich and poor. Factors such as freedom of travel and owning property (in some cases large enough to house the church) show that some members were well off. Mention of slaves, on the other hand, implies that some were poor. That being the case, the issue of food takes on a new dimension, for the main opportunity for the poor to eat meat was at the great public festivals, which would certainly have involved pagan rites. Thus to take the stance that Christians should not eat such meat would mean that the poor would never eat meat at all. But for the rich, who could eat meat at home, it might be no more than a minor inconvenience.

Likewise with the Lord's supper. Sunday was not a special day for the Roman world and so those who worked for others would have to negotiate time off in order to come to a church meeting. Slaves could only attend after they had done all that their master required and would probably find themselves arriving late. And what did they find when they arrived at this celebration of Christian unity? That those hosting the meal and those whose working life permitted them to arrive early had consumed all the best food. Theissen says: 'The core of the problem was that wealthier Christians made it plain to all just how much the rest were dependent on them, dependent on the generosity of those who were better off. Differences in menu are a relatively timeless symbol of status and wealth, and those not so well off came face to face with their own social inferiority at a most basic level.'[9] As an example, he quotes an amusing speech by Martial, who complains to his host:

> Since I am asked to dinner, no longer, as before, a purchased guest, why is not the same dinner served to me as to you? You take oysters fattened in the Lucrine lake, I suck a mussel through a hole in the shell; you get mushrooms, I take hog funguses; you tackle turbot, but I brill. Golden with fat, a turtledove gorges you with its bloated rump; there is set before me a magpie that has died in its cage. Why do I dine without you although, Ponticus, I am dining with you?[10]

If Theissen is correct, then it places the description of the supper (1 Cor 11:23–26) in a different light. Paul did not cite the last supper tradition in order to make some doctrinal point about the nature of the elements or the frequency of celebration but to call to mind that solemn occasion when Jesus shared bread and wine with *all* who were present. This is contrary to how the well-off were behaving, who are warned: 'So then, my brothers and sisters, when you come together to eat, wait for one another. If you are hungry, eat at home, so that when you come together, it will not be for your condemnation' (11:33–34). Such a statement makes clear that Paul is aiming his comments mainly at the rich, for it would be an insult to tell slaves that they could eat any time they like 'at home'.

Another example is the different emphases that we find between early and late documents in the New Testament. One way of explaining this is to talk about theological development (we did this with the Gospels) but this ignores important social factors. Thus, whether we are talking about the Church or any group or club, there is always a significant difference between the culture of the pioneers and that of the second and third generations. Max Weber, the great sociologist, spoke of the early phase as 'charismatic'. Everything is new and exciting. There is an emphasis on spontaneity, with rules and regulations invented 'on the hoof', as and when necessary. But eventually, the pioneers die (or leave) and others have to take their place. There follows a process which Weber called 'routinization', where a number of questions have to be clarified: What does the movement stand for? How do people join? What are the conditions of membership? What behaviour is unacceptable? In other words, the movement becomes an institution.

Does this help to explain the New Testament documents? Though there is some dispute about dating, the earliest documents in the New Testament are Thessalonians, Galatians and Corinthians. In each of these there is vigour and excitement. Jesus is expected soon (1 Thess 4:17; 1 Cor 7:29). The Spirit is powerfully operative (Gal 3:5; 1 Cor 12 – 14) and the only mention of leaders is a reference to those 'who have charge of you' (1 Thess 5:12). However, in the Pastoral epistles (1 and 2 Timothy, Titus) we appear to be breathing a different atmosphere. There is an emphasis on order, holding firm to the traditions and faithfully transmitting them to the next generation. There are instructions about enrolling widows, who have to be over sixty and married only once (1 Tim 5:9). Specific leaders are mentioned (elders, deacons, bishops), together with lists of requirements that each must satisfy. There is very little mention of the Spirit, the return of Jesus or an 'every member' ministry.

In between these early and late documents are the epistles to the Colossians and Ephesians. The exact date is disputed, partly because of the features we are about to mention. Thus, while differing from the Pastoral epistles, they do show signs of routinization. For example, both contain household codes for ordering family life and employment (Col 3:18 – 4:1; Eph 5:22 – 6:8). Both speak of the Church as a universal phenomenon as well as a local congregation. And the image of being the body of Christ is different from that of Romans and 1 Corinthians. In the latter, Christians are likened to parts of the body ('The eye cannot say to the hand'), but, in Colossians and Ephesians, the metaphor is now that Christ is the head of the body.

For many, these differences have resulted in a very negative picture of the later epistles, where all the vigour seems to have gone. Indeed, modern house churches that speak of 'returning to the New Testament church' are seldom thinking of the Pastoral epistles. It is the communal sharing in Acts or the charismatic 'every member' ministry of Corinthians that is usually in mind. But if we consider them in the light of Max Weber's analysis of society (*The Theory of Social and Economic Organization*, 1947), they become more understandable. Pioneer movements do change in the second and third generations. Indeed, had there not been an emphasis on 'guarding the deposit' and 'appointing elders', we would probably not have a New Testament at all. Social-scientific study is a branch of historical criticism which challenges many previous reconstructions by emphasizing the social nature of texts.

Conclusion

Historical research that only focused on the sources behind the texts ran out of steam in the 1950s. It was replaced by a concern for the authors themselves and the circumstances that caused them to write. Claims of what Jesus said or thought were problematic because of the nature of the sources. But studies on 'Matthew's view of the Church' or 'Luke's view of riches' seemed to be on much firmer ground. The Gospels are primary evidence for the outlook of the authors and only secondary evidence for the outlook of Jesus. However, while such studies continue to pour from the presses, the 1980s saw another approach to the Bible take root. This is usually referred to as the 'literary approach', though this term covers a wide variety of methods. In terms of our diagram, it marks a return to the vertical dimension but without the Church looming in the background. The key questions were: How do texts affect readers and how do readers affect or make sense of texts?

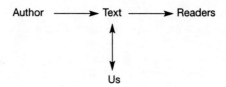

FURTHER READING

An interesting attempt to present the theology of the four Gospels in
the light of the ancient symbols (Lion, Ox, Eagle, Human) is found in
R. A. Burridge, *Four Gospels, One Jesus* (SPCK, 1994). And for a
detailed discussion of the picture of Christ in each of the Gospels, see
Rudolf Schnackenburg's *Jesus in the Gospels: A Biblical Christology*
(John Knox Press, 1995). Redaction criticism is not much practised in
Old Testament studies because of the difficulties of identifying an
author but see J. Barton's *Reading the Old Testament: Method in Biblical
Study* (Darton, Longman and Todd/Westminster, 1984). And for a
social-scientific approach to Paul, see Wayne Meeks, *The First Urban
Christians: The Social World of the Apostle Paul* (Yale University Press,
1983).

NOTES

1. Translated as Martin Dibelius, *From Tradition to Gospel* (J. Clark, 1971) and R.
   Bultmann, *The History of the Synoptic Tradition* (Blackwell, 1968).
2. This title was obviously thought to be too obscure for the English-speaking
   world. The English title is *The Theology of Saint Luke* (Faber/Harper, 1960).
3. M. Borg, *Jesus in Contemporary Scholarship* (Trinity Press International, 1994),
   p. 151.
4. Ibid.
5. D. Nineham, *Saint Mark* (Penguin Books, 1963), p. 33.
6. M. D. Hooker, *The Message of Mark* (Epworth Press, 1983), p. 121.
7. C. Blomberg, *The Historical Reliability of the Gospels* (Inter-Varsity Press,
   1987), p. 41.
8. G. R. Osborne, 'Redaction criticism' in *Dictionary of Jesus and the Gospels*
   (Inter-Varsity Press, 1992).
9. G. Theissen,*The Social Setting of Pauline Christianity* (T. & T. Clark, 1982), p.
   160.
10. Ibid., p. 157.

4

How do texts affect readers?

Though the benefits of historical criticism have been immense, a grave weakness was that it focused on discovering what the text meant *then* – to the detriment of what it might mean to readers *today*. Ordinary Christians, praying over the Scriptures and declaring what God had shown them, were regarded by 'critical' scholars as naive. Furthermore, those who appealed to the Scriptures in doctrinal or moral debate were regarded as guilty of misusing the Bible because they failed to consider the original intention of the author. For those who were schooled in the historical method, even the claim to be a follower of Christ was complicated by questions such as: Did he really say that? Did he really institute a eucharist? Did he really think of himself as the Messiah? In short, the Enlightenment spirit, which attempted to free the text from the dogmatic control of the Church, had ended up by placing it within the dogmatic control of the professional historian.

In reaction to this, scholarship swung in the 1980s to the question of how texts affect readers and how readers affect or make sense of texts. Historical study was quite clear that the individual authors of Scripture had their own point of view and this must be taken into account when analysing their texts. However, the same is also true of modern readers (and modern scholars). No one comes to the text from a neutral or objective stance: all come with certain presuppositions and interests and this inevitably colours what is found. Yet for Christians, one of the reasons for reading the Bible is the belief that it is able to challenge and transform, as we saw in our first chapter. The study of how texts affect readers and how readers affect texts is sometimes called reader-response criticism. Sanders and Davies (*Studying the Synoptic Gospels*, 1989) explain:

> Reader-response criticism explores the dialectic of text and reader.
> On the one hand, the text controls the reader's response through its

own strategies and conventions, selecting and arranging from contingencies those matters and patterns which it requires the reader to notice. On the other hand, the reader must actualize the world of the text in such a way as to be moved and enlightened by it. Some reader-response critics pay more attention to the strategies of the text and some to the psychology of the reader.[1]

In this chapter, we shall focus on the first of these, the question of how texts affect readers. In our next chapter we shall consider the other side of the interaction, how readers affect or make sense of texts.

The process of reading

Before we can even begin to read the Bible or any other book, we must have a basic vocabulary and set of meanings. Otherwise, it will simply be squiggles on a page (or electronic data). This becomes clear as soon as you remember that the original texts were not written in English. You could have a page of the Hebrew Old Testament in front of you and could reverently declare it to be the 'word of God', but unless you have some experience of this 'right to left' language, it will remain 'non-sense' to you. Interpretation is only possible if you come to a text with a basic set of meanings and experiences. For example, suppose you are reading Paul's letter to the Romans (in English) and you come across the word 'sin'. Now depending on your previous reading and experiences, this may suggest to you one or more of the following:

1. gross immorality or wickedness (hence nothing to do with you);
2. letting God down or failure (we do it all the time);
3. letting ourselves down (we do it some of the time);
4. injustice, such as being part of an economic system that keeps third world countries in poverty (some are aware of this, others are not);
5. an old-fashioned expression ('living in sin') which society now finds quaint.

Whatever 'sin' means to you, your first attempt to understand what Paul is saying has to start with that. These are your first thoughts or impressions on the passage. However, if you are a careful reader, you might find that you are forced to revise these initial meanings. For example, Paul declares in Romans 3:23 that 'all have sinned and fall short of the glory of God'. Now it is clear that not everyone has committed gross immorality, so that, if that was your starting-point, you might be challenged to revise it (or you could declare Paul to be wrong; not everyone has sinned and fallen short of the glory of God). In this way, the text *can* speak back to you. Some interpretations fit the passage better than others. Of course it cannot *force* you to change your mind and the verb 'speak' here is clearly figurative. But if you continue to ignore such prompts, your reading of the text will become problematic and eventually create dissonance. On the other hand, if you are prepared to modify what you thought 'sin' meant, your next reading of Romans will take place with a revised set of meanings. The following diagram illustrates the process:

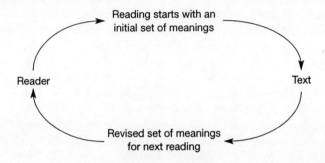

Rhetorical criticism

In the ancient world, the art of persuasion was called rhetoric and a number of prominent Christians (Tertullian, Cyprian, Augustine) were rhetoricians before they were Christians. Rhetorical criticism (some would prefer the term rhetorical analysis) is the study of how texts influence readers. What literary devices are used in order to persuade readers to accept the author's point of view? It is particularly relevant to those parts of the Bible which record speeches or oracles. For example, consider the summons in Isaiah 1:18:

> Come now, let us argue it out, says the Lord:
> though your sins are like scarlet,
> they shall be like snow;
> though they are red like crimson,
> they shall become like wool.

The oracle invites the hearers to consider their present state and hope for something better. At the moment, their sins are like scarlet, red or crimson (perhaps a reference to blood). But this could be different; they could be like snow or wool. The meaning of the metaphor becomes clearer from its use in other passages. For example, in Daniel's vision of God, he describes the glorious figure as having clothes as 'white as snow' and the 'hair of his head like pure wool' (Dan 7:9). This is picked up in the book of Revelation where John says Christ's 'head and his hair were white as white wool, white as snow' (Rev 1:14). The hearers are invited to imagine an enormous change in their situation, from blood-red sins to pure snowy-white. But there is more:

> If you are willing and obedient,
> you shall eat the good of the land;
> but if you refuse and rebel,
> you shall be devoured by the sword;
> for the mouth of the Lord has spoken. (Isa 1:19–20)

Having whetted their appetite for such a transformation, the conditions are now laid out. One way involves obedience and a further promise is given: 'you shall eat the good of the land'. The other way is the way of rebellion and a threat is added: 'you shall be devoured by the sword'. Thus the oracle uses at least three rhetorical devices to persuade. First, there is an appeal to the imagination: think how it would be to have your blood-red sins transformed into something as pure as snow. Second, there is promise: 'you shall eat the good of the land'. Third, there is threat: 'you shall be devoured by the sword'. And, if that is not enough, the oracle continues by highlighting their predicament: 'How the faithful city has become a whore! She that was full of justice, righteousness lodged in her – but now murderers! Your silver has become dross, your wine is mixed with water' (1:21–22).

Another rhetorical device is to carry on a dialogue with an imaginary inquisitor who supplies you with questions. These not only anticipate possible objections to the speaker's position; they also allow him or her to answer them when they are ready. Thus, in Paul's letter to the Romans, the argument is punctuated by such questions as:

> Then what advantage has the Jew? (3:1)
> What then? Are we any better off? (3:9)
> Then what becomes of boasting? (3:27)
> What then are we to say was gained by Abraham... ? (4:1)
> Is this blessedness, then, pronounced only on the circumcised... ? (4:9)
> Should we continue in sin in order that grace may abound? (6:1)
> Should we sin because we are not under law but under grace? (6:15)

Paul knows that unless he can offer satisfactory answers to these questions, his message will not be convincing. But he only wants to answer them when he is ready, that is, when he has got to the relevant part of the argument. Thus, in 6:15, the questioner asks: 'Should we sin because we are not under law but under grace?' It is a dilemma many Christians have found themselves in. At the moment of temptation, does the message of forgiveness offer sufficient incentive to resist? But forgiveness is not the sum total of the Gospel message. Becoming a Christian involves a transfer of loyalties: 'For just as you once presented your members as slaves to impurity and to greater and greater iniquity, so now present your members as slaves to righteousness for sanctification' (6:19). And Paul is quite happy to mention the incentives of reward and punishment: 'For the wages of sin is death, but the free gift of God is eternal life in Christ Jesus our Lord' (6:23). But the latter phrase shows that it is not an abstract promise of reward that acts as incentive. It is rooted in the object of the Christian's new loyalty, 'Christ Jesus our Lord'.

Rhetorical criticism then is the study of the means whereby an author seeks to convince or persuade readers to accept a particular point of view. It is therefore close to the aims and goals of redaction criticism. If we agree with the point of view we congratulate the author on his or her rhetorical skill. We admire his or her ability to 'make a case', to present arguments clearly, to give good illustrations, indeed, to communicate. But it is sobering to remember that, if we do not agree with the position being offered, we usually refer to it as manipulation. The author tries to control the reader's responses by various clever devices. How we view it (including the Bible) depends on whether we are disposed to accept the point of view being offered.

Narrative

Rhetorical criticism of speeches and oracles is close to redaction criticism's concern with authors. But when we turn to stories, we are less concerned with authors and more concerned with the dynamics of the text itself. How is it that stories can have such a dramatic impact on readers? Even when they are not literally true, like Jesus' parables? Anthony Thiselton (*New Horizons in Hermeneutics*, 1992) suggests the following reasons:

1. Biblical stories catch us off-guard

When we read stories, we sometimes get so involved with the characters that the ending can have a huge emotional impact on us. Had the author stated the point right at the beginning, we might have been impervious to it, but we were taken along by the story. The author got behind our natural defences by luring us into their story world. Just for a while, we suspended life in the present world to live in the world of the story. In short, we were caught off-guard. An excellent example of this occurs in 2 Samuel 12. David has committed adultery with

Bathsheba and then plotted to have her husband killed. Nathan approaches him and tells him a story:

> There were two men in a certain city, the one rich and the other poor. The rich man had very many flocks and herds; but the poor man had nothing but one little ewe lamb, which he had bought. He brought it up, and it grew up with him and with his children; it used to eat of his meagre fare, and drink from his cup, and lie in his bosom, and it was like a daughter to him. Now there came a traveller to the rich man, and he was loathe to take one of his own flock or herd to prepare for the wayfarer who had come to him, but he took the poor man's lamb, and prepared that for the guest who had come to him. (2 Sam 12:1–4)

The story is vivid and has an immediate impact on David. He declares 'As the Lord lives, the man who has done this deserves to die; he shall restore the lamb fourfold, because he did this thing, and because he had no pity'. But then comes the punch line. Nathan declares:

> You are the man! Thus says the Lord, the God of Israel: I anointed you king over Israel, and I rescued you from the hand of Saul; I gave you your master's house, and your master's wives into your bosom, and gave you the house of Israel and of Judah; and if that had been too little, I would have added as much more. Why have you despised the word of the Lord, to do what is evil in his sight? You have struck down Uriah the Hittite with the sword, and have taken his wife to be your wife... (2 Sam 12:7–9)

David was caught off-guard, as are countless readers of other parts of the Bible. Thiselton explains: 'Because the narrative entices them into its world and enthrals them, they become unconsciously exposed to viewpoints, judgments, and reversals of assumptions which in other modes of discourse would have called explicitly for conscious willingness to be "open" and to "listen to the text". Narrative can *reverse expectations which initially would be hostile* to its viewpoint.'[2]

Thiselton's insight offers an alternative way of looking at the parables of Jesus. Consider again the parable of the Good Samaritan. The lawyer has successfully answered Jesus' question by declaring that eternal life comes from loving God with all your heart, soul, strength and mind and your neighbour as yourself (Luke 10:27). But he wishes clarification: 'And who is my neighbour?' Now Jesus could have answered him 'Anyone in need', but he elects to tell a story:

> A man was going down from Jerusalem to Jericho, and fell into the

hands of robbers, who stripped him, beat him, and went away, leaving him half dead.

Historians tell us that the road from Jerusalem to Jericho was notorious for this sort of thing. The man may well have thought that Jesus was recounting a true story. He continues:

> Now by chance a priest was going down that road; and when he saw him, he passed by on the other side. So likewise a Levite, when he came to the place and saw him, passed by on the other side.

The mention of priest and Levite is surprising. This is beginning to sound like an anti-clerical story. No doubt the next person will be a lay person, who will show the sort of compassion that the clergy should have shown. But the lawyer is in for an even greater surprise:

> But a Samaritan while travelling came near him; and when he saw him, he was moved with pity. He went to him and bandaged his wounds, having poured oil and wine on them. Then he put him on his own animal, brought him to an inn, and took care of him. The next day he took out two denarii, gave them to the innkeeper, and said, 'Take care of him; and when I come back, I will repay you whatever more you spend.'

Despite being able to recite the commandments, the lawyer probably had little love for Samaritans (Jews did not associate with Samaritans, as we are told in John 4:9). Jesus asks him 'Which of these three, do you think, was a neighbour to the man who fell into the hands of the robbers?' There is only one answer and the lawyer must bow to the logic of the story. The one who acted as neighbour is the one 'who showed him mercy'. Jesus ends with 'Go and do likewise'. Thus the man is not only given a poignant example of love; he is also confronted with his own prejudice. Loving one's neighbour is of little use if it is not willing to cross racial barriers. We are not told what his response was but he probably did not forget the story in a hurry.

2. Biblical stories embody truth in people/characters

It is a common experience that knowing about someone is not the same as actually knowing them. Indeed, it is possible to know someone intimately (partner, relative, flat-mate) without being able to list very many 'facts' about them (height, weight, colour of eyes, etc.). Though the Church thought it necessary to use doctrinal statements to distinguish truth from error (i.e. the creeds), most Christians 'know' Jesus from the stories about him (and their own personal experience).

For example, the author of John's Gospel could have simply told us that we should serve one another. Narrating the story of the foot-washing (John 13) is much more powerful because it embeds a powerful image in the mind.

3. Biblical stories stimulate imagination

Doctrinal statements often function as a test of orthodoxy and can be either accepted or rejected. Historical reconstructions are a matter of probabilities. Stories, on the other hand, invite imagination and exploration. Though we are not always conscious of it, when we read a story we are always filling in gaps. We build up a picture of the characters and the settings. We imagine what it must have been like for Peter to deny Christ or the woman with the issue of blood to touch Jesus' garment. We are not told these things in the text but they are necessary in order to bring the story to life. We find ourselves liking some characters and disliking others. We speculate on why certain characters act as they do and how things might have been different. This leads on to Thiselton's fourth point.

4. Biblical stories invite participation

Getting involved in a story involves our own story. We identify with certain characters. Why? Perhaps because we see echoes of our own upbringing or conversion in one of them. We see traits described that are typical of ourselves and hence see 'our story' in the narrative story. A good example of this can be found in the *Spiritual Exercises* of St Ignatius, where you are invited to imagine yourself into the story. For example, on the last supper, he says:

> The first Point is to see the persons of the Supper, and, reflecting on myself, to see to drawing some profit from them.
>
> The second, to hear what they are talking about, and likewise to draw some profit from it.
>
> The third, to look at what they are doing, and draw some profit.
>
> The fourth, to consider that which Christ our Lord is suffering in His Humanity, or wants to suffer, according to the passage which is being contemplated, and here to commence with much vehemence and to force myself to grieve, be sad and weep, and so to labor through the other points which follow.
>
> The fifth, to consider how the Divinity hides Itself, that is, how It

could destroy Its enemies and does not do it, and how It leaves the most sacred Humanity to suffer so very cruelly.

The sixth, to consider how He suffers all this for my sins, etc.; and what I ought to do and suffer for Him.[3]

Literary studies have identified a number of features that affect the way we read a story. For example, we are taken through a story by a narrator. Consider the following verses from John's Gospel:

But he was speaking of the temple of his body. (2:21)

He said this to test him, for he himself knew what he was going to do. (6:6)

He was speaking of Judas son of Simon Iscariot, for he, though one of the twelve, was going to betray him. (6:71)

Now he said this about the Spirit, which believers in him were to receive; (7:39)

They did not understand that he was speaking to them about the Father. (8:27)

He said this to indicate the kind of death he was to die. (12:33)

For he knew who was to betray him; (13:11)

This was to fulfill what Jesus had said when he indicated the kind of death he was to die. (18:32)

He said this to indicate the kind of death by which he would glorify God. (21:19)

So the rumour spread in the community that this disciple would not die. Yet Jesus did not say to him that he would not die, (21:23)

These are not part of the story as such but asides to the reader. They guide us through the story and since the narrator (normally) seems so good at making sense of the events described, we are well disposed to accept the points of view being offered. These might be explicit, as in the doctrinal assertions of chapter 1 ('In the beginning was the Word, and the Word was with God, and the Word was God') or implicit, as in the following:

Because of this many of his disciples turned back and no longer went about with him. So Jesus asked the twelve, 'Do you also wish to go away?' Simon Peter answered him, 'Lord, to whom can we go? You have the words of eternal life. We have come to believe and know that you are the Holy One of God.' (John 6:66–69)

We are not forced to take the stance that Peter takes. We could disagree with the point of view being offered but that is to place ourselves with those that found the teaching too difficult. In actual fact, it may be nothing of the kind but the flow of the narrative has encouraged us to accept the story and the values it is propagating. Why doubt now? A good illustration of the effect of a narrative comment is found in Jesus' sayings about what defiles a person.

Mark 7:18–19	Matthew 15:17–19
'Do you not see that whatever goes into a person from outside cannot defile, since it enters, not the heart but the stomach, and goes out into the sewer?' *(Thus he declared all foods clean.)* ...	'Do you not see that whatever goes into the mouth enters the stomach, and goes out into the sewer?
'It is what comes out of a person that defiles. For it is from within, from the human heart, that evil intentions come: fornication, theft, murder...'	But what comes out of the mouth proceeds from the heart, and this is what defiles. For out of the heart come evil intentions, murder...'

The passages are very similar except that Mark has the narrative comment 'Thus he declared all foods clean'. Whether this was Jesus' intention cannot be decided but the narrative comment makes it clear that we are supposed to take it this way. Thus the same tradition is being used to make different points. Matthew keeps to the spirit of the saying which contrasts the actions of the heart with external actions. But Mark turns it into a specific ruling for his community, namely, that the Old Testament food laws are no longer in force. A similar thing is observable with the parable of the lost sheep, which appears in Matthew 18:10–14 and Luke 15:3–7.

The effect of being taken through a story by a narrator is that we are often oblivious of the fact that the narrator appears to be both omniscient (knows everything) and omnipresent (can be everywhere). For example, the narrator is able to tell us what is going on in Jesus' mind. Consider these comments from John's Gospel:

When Jesus realized that they were about to come and take him by force (6:15)
For Jesus knew from the first who were the ones that did not believe, (6:64)
Jesus knew that they wanted to ask him, (16:19)
Then Jesus, knowing all that was to happen to him, (18:4)
After this, when Jesus knew that all was now finished, (19:28)

Also, the narrator is always present where the action is. If Jesus is at the well (John 4), the narrator is there to record the conversation. When the woman returns to the town, the narrator is there to hear her report, while simultaneously being back at the well to tell us what the disciples had to say. It is a measure of the skill of the author that we do not question how this can be so. Think how different the Gospels would be if we read 'And the disciples returned to Jesus but I have been unable to discover what was said'. Our confidence in the narrator is shown in passages like John 3:11–36. Verse 11 begins with Jesus' reply to Nicodemus ('Very truly, I tell you, we speak of what we know'). But it is unclear whether the paragraph that begins at verse 16 ('For God so loved the world') or verse 17 ('Indeed, God did not send the Son into the world to condemn') continues Jesus' words or whether they are commentary provided by the narrator (the original manuscripts contain no punctuation).

Likewise with the end of the chapter. John the Baptist is speaking in 3:27: 'No one can receive anything except what has been given from heaven. You yourselves are my witnesses that I said, "I am not the Messiah, but I have been sent ahead of him."' But is it John or the narrator who is speaking at the end of the paragraph: 'Whoever believes in the Son has eternal life; whoever disobeys the Son will not see life, but must endure God's wrath'? The point is that, whether John said it or not, it hardly matters to most readers, for the narrator has convinced us that he is utterly reliable. Whether Jesus, John or the author of the Gospel is speaking, they all speak as one (and use the same language and style). While the lack of punctuation in the original means that it is sometimes impossible to tell when one voice stops and another starts, for most readers it makes no difference.

Plot

Plot may simply be the chronological sequence of events (as far as the author knows it) but the differences between the Gospels suggest that this is not their leading feature. Alan Culpepper (*Anatomy of the Fourth Gospel*, 1983)[4] says that though the Evangelists received traditions about Jesus, they still had to fashion them into a coherent whole. The resulting sequence (plot) has a significant effect on the reader. For example, in the Synoptic Gospels, the cleansing of the temple forms a fitting climax to the clashes between Jesus and the Jewish leaders. According to Mark, there are mutterings of blasphemy as early as the second chapter (2:7), leading to a plot to kill him in the third (3:6). Yet Jesus continues his ministry, travelling up and down the country, preaching and teaching, healing and exorcizing demons. There are further disputes in chapters 7 and 8 (see 7:5; 8:11) which come to a climax in chapter 11, with his entry into Jerusalem and the cleansing of the temple (11:15–19). From here on, the narrative is swift, with disputes in chapter 12, apocalyptic discourse in chapter 13 and his arrest in chapter 14. In the flow of Mark's story, it is the cleansing of the temple which finally precipitates Jesus' arrest and death.

However, this is clearly not the case in John's Gospel since the cleansing comes right at the beginning (John 2:13–22). Its different setting gives it a different function. One suggestion is that the author is trying to illustrate the verse in the prologue which says 'He came to what was his own, and his own people did not accept him' (1:11). He does this by narrating a number of 'transfer' stories. First is the water into wine, illustrating the superiority of Christianity (2:1–11). Second is the cleansing of the temple, indicating God's judgement on Israel (2:13–22). Third is the story of Nicodemus (a leading Jew), who will only see the kingdom if he is born again (3:1–10). Thus John's story (plot) presents a break between Jesus and Judaism right from the beginning.

Experience shows that certain types of plot tend to produce certain types of reaction. For example, most stories have some sort of hero and this character can either succeed or fail. If he or she succeeds (the happy ending), readers are usually pleased. Providing it is not contrived or unbelievable, most of us like a happy ending and this goes far deeper than wishful thinking. There is something deep down that expects good things to happen to good people. It is reassuring. On the other hand, if the hero fails, this is deeply unsettling. Books that lead you to identify with heroes only to kill them off are often subversive. They are intending to challenge your apathy or traditional values.

Further, most plots usually have a villain or bad person. Generally speaking, we do not expect them to prosper for that would go against our sense of fairness or justice. That is why the psalmist cries out to God when the wicked prosper. This is not how it should be! Conversely, we are pleased when the wicked get what they deserve. We may have radically different views about punishment but few people want to see the wicked 'getting away with it'. Think how different the Gospels would be if they ended with Judas living happily on his thirty pieces of silver.

All this can be utilized by an author. Stories generally move in either an upward direction ('rags to riches') or downward (tragedy) and this has a predictable effect on the reader. Within this framework, interest is often focused on the reasons for success or failure. For example, why did Judas betray Jesus? Was it a moment of weakness or a flaw in his character? In Mark, the betrayal of Jesus comes completely out of the blue. It is inexplicable and hence a little worrying. After all, if one of the twelve can be with Jesus for so long and still fall, where does that leave us? But John takes care of this. Not only are we told that Jesus knew this would happen (6:71; 13:11); we are also told that Judas was a thief and used to help himself from the common purse (12:6). Whether there is any historical basis for such a claim is open to debate. But what is clear is that John has made an awkward incident (for the reader) into an understandable and hence less disturbing one.

Irony

Amongst the various literary devices open to an author, irony has been thought to play a significant role in biblical stories. A dictionary definition is a 'device whereby a character in a play or book says something which has one meaning for him and a deeper one only visible to audience or reader'.[5] A good example is the speech of Caiaphas in John's Gospel:

> So the chief priests and the Pharisees called a meeting of the council, and said, 'What are we to do? This man is performing many signs. If we let him go on like this, everyone will believe in him, and the Romans will come and destroy both our holy place and our nation.' But one of them, Caiaphas, who was high priest that year, said to them, 'You know nothing at all! You do not understand that it is better for you to have one man die for the people than to have the whole nation destroyed.' (John 11:47–50)

Caiaphas is talking about getting rid of Christ as a political expedient but the reader knows that Jesus did in fact 'die for the people'. It is as if the author is giving the reader a knowing look or nudge. They share a secret unknown to the characters in the story and this gives us confidence that the author knows what he is talking about. The prologues of the Gospels function in a similar way. Each in its own way serves to put the reader in the picture. For example, we are prepared for the Nicodemus dialogue about being 'born again' (John 3:1–10) by the statement in the prologue: 'But to all who received him, who believed in his name, he gave power to become children of God, who were born, not of blood or of the will of the flesh or of the will of man, but of God' (John 1:12–13). With this knowledge, we can only smile at Nicodemus' stupidity as he enquires: 'How can anyone be born after having grown old? Can one enter a second time into the mother's womb and be born?' (3:4). But this is more than a piece of amusement for it is part of the plot. Who is Nicodemus? The chapter opens with the words: 'Now there was a Pharisee named Nicodemus, *a leader of the Jews.*' The reader is urged to take a negative view of the Pharisees and a superior view of Jesus.

Conclusion

It should now be clear that there is a fundamental difference between historical and literary approaches to the Bible. A historical approach seeks meaning in the original context, whether this is the actual events being narrated or the intention of the author. In effect, the text is treated as a window to something behind it. And it is that something which is the real focus of attention. Literary approaches, however, focus on the actual text and its interaction with readers. Whether what is written corresponds exactly to what happened or to an author's intention is always a matter of debate. The text is what we have in front of us and its influence depends on a variety of rhetorical and literary devices such as plot, an imaginary questioner or a narrator. The 1980s saw a proliferation of studies with titles like *Matthew As Story* (Kingsbury) or *Mark As Story* (Rhoads and Michie), each trying to illuminate the dynamic between text and reader.

But are such studies grounded in anything objective? Do all people, across time and culture, respond to irony in the same way? Does everyone find a happy ending fulfilling? Do texts really have this power to influence? In our next chapter, we consider how readers make sense of texts. For a growing number of scholars, the most influential factor in determining meaning is what readers themselves bring to the text. That is why historical reconstructions vary so much and why scholars disagree about literary structure. The background of the reader, what they know and why they are reading the text, has been left out of most interpretations of the Bible since the Enlightenment. Yet where you stand greatly affects what you see and hence how you interpret. As we shall see.

FURTHER READING

Discussion of all the biblical books from a literary point of view can be found in the very reasonably priced *The Literary Guide to the Bible,* ed. R. Alter and F. Kermode (Harvard University Press/Collins, 1987). Also useful are their separate works: R. Alter, *The Art of Biblical Narrative* (Basic Books/Allen and Unwin, 1981) and F. Kermode, *The Genesis of Secrecy: On the Interpretation of Narrative* (Harvard University Press, 1979). Fortress Press have been particularly prominent in publishing books on literary approaches. For an introduction, see Mark Allen Powell's *What Is Narrative Criticism?* (1990). On individual books, Alan Culpepper's *Anatomy of the Fourth Gospel* (1983) and *Mark As Story* (D. Rhoads and D. Michie, 1982) remain classics. For the Old Testament, see the two books by David

Gunn, *The Story of King David* (1978) and *The Fate of King Saul* (1980), both by Sheffield Academic Press.

NOTES

1. *Studying the Synoptic Gospels*, ed. E. P. Sanders and M. Davies (SCM, 1989), p. 240.
2. A. C.Thiselton, *New Horizons in Hermeneutics* (HarperCollins, 1992), p. 567.
3. D. L. Fleming SJ, *The Spiritual Exercises of Saint Ignatius: A Literal Translation and a Contemporary Reading* (The Institute of Jesuit Resources, 1980), pp. 116–18.
4. A. Culpepper, *Anatomy of the Fourth Gospel: A Study in Literary Design* (Fortress Press, 1983), ch. 4. Much of the material in this chapter is drawn from this book.
5. *The Penguin English Dictionary* (2nd edn, 1969), p. 398.

5

How do readers affect texts?

We have so far focused on how texts affect readers. The other side of that interaction is how readers affect or make sense of texts. For example, depending on whether you are rich or poor, you will inevitably see passages about 'poverty and riches' in a different light. The entrepreneur quotes the parable of the talents to justify enterprise and risk (Matt 25:14–30). In the parable, those who used their money to make more money were commended but the one who was afraid and simply buried his talent was rebuked ('you ought to have invested my money with the bankers, and on my return I would have received what was my own with interest'). On the other hand, the socialist quotes the parable of the workers where the man who only worked one hour was still paid a living wage (Matt 20:1–16). The problem is that while we see this in others, we are often blind to it in ourselves. One of the key ideas in modern study is that there is no such thing as 'neutral' interpretation. How it looks always depends on where you stand.

Liberation readings

Much of our language about God is to do with power. We speak of 'Lord' and 'King'. Many prayers begin with the words 'Almighty God'. We talk of 'dominion' and 'majesty'. We use the male pronoun 'He'. Yet for the Christian, what God is like is seen most clearly in Christ who 'came not to be served but to serve, and to give his life a ransom for many' (Mark 10:45). Does God desire power while Christ delights to serve? Should we not reinterpret our idea of God in the light of the revelation of Christ? Or does the Church like the idea of a God who wishes to dominate because it authenticates its own desire to dominate? Liberation theology suggests that traditional formulations of Christianity are deficient in that they are produced by the powerful (synods, conferences, universities etc.) for the powerful. And those holding power have a vested interest in producing interpretations that preserve the *status quo* rather than challenging it. As Moltmann (*The Crucified God*, 1974) asks: 'Which God motivates Christian faith: the crucified God or the gods of religion, race and class?'[1]

For many evangelicals, it has seemed self-evident that the main message of the Bible is individual salvation. We have all sinned and fall short of the glory of God. We are all worthy of judgement and can do nothing to save ourselves. So God did something. He sent Jesus to die on the cross for our sins. The debt has been paid so that anyone who turns to Christ and puts their trust in him will be saved. Of course, Christians have a responsibility to love their neighbours and act as salt and light in society. But that is secondary. The main message of the Bible is that Jesus died for our sins so that we might go to heaven. And the main task of the Christian is to proclaim that message so that others might join us there.

Those who differed from this and actively tried to change society were criticized as preaching a 'social gospel'. They were accused of mistaking bodily needs for spiritual needs and diverting Christians from their true task of evangelizing the world. But, increasingly, Christians who do not live in the affluent West have challenged this exclusive emphasis on individual salvation because:

(a) it does not do justice to the message of Jesus. There is far more in the Gospels about poverty and social justice than there is about individuals being 'saved';

(b) it is the sort of interpretation one would expect from a group of people who are living very comfortably and therefore have no desire to change society.

In regard to the first, consider these extracts from the Magnificat, the Nazareth sermon and the ending of Matthew 25:

He has shown strength with his arm; he has scattered the proud in the thoughts of their hearts. He has brought down the powerful from their thrones, and lifted up the lowly; he has filled the hungry with good things, and sent the rich away empty. (Luke 1:51–53)

The Spirit of the Lord is upon me, because he has anointed me to bring good news to the poor. He has sent me to proclaim release to the captives and recovery of sight to the blind, to let the oppressed go free, to proclaim the year of the Lord's favour. (Luke 4:18)

Then they also will answer, 'Lord, when was it that we saw you hungry or thirsty or a stranger or naked or sick or in prison, and did not take care of you?' Then he will answer them, 'Truly I tell you, just as you did not do it to one of the least of these, you did not do it to me.' (Matt 25:44–45)

With this in mind, many of the key passages cited in evangelistic campaigns take on new meaning. For example, the so-called 'great commission' passage reads: 'Go therefore and make disciples of all nations, baptizing them in the name of the Father and of the Son and of the Holy Spirit, and teaching them to obey everything that I have commanded you' (Matt 28:19–20). This has been taken as a command to gain converts, to tell individuals that their sins can be forgiven. But, in the light of the above passages, one might question whether this really does justice to the context. Is it not more likely that the meaning of 'disciple' here refers to one who follows Jesus and does the sort of things mentioned in the above passages?

One of the verses most often given as a gospel invitation is Revelation 3:20: 'Listen! I am standing at the door, knocking; if you hear my voice and open the door, I will come in to you and eat with you, and you with me.' Taken out of context, the words offer an excellent promise of individual salvation. Jesus is knocking on the door of your heart. If you open the door to him, he will come into your life and begin a relationship with you. But is that what the verse is really about? It comes in that section of the book of Revelation where messages are given to seven churches. In this case, it is the church at Laodicea, which is described as lukewarm and complacent. Revelation 3:19 tells them to repent and then 3:20 offers the picture of Jesus standing outside the church and knocking. If they let him in, he will dine with them and be part (once again) of their corporate life.

I have a friend who became a Christian at a Billy Graham crusade and I was the person appointed to 'follow him up'. He tells me that one of the things that helped him most was when I pointed him to Philippians 1:6: 'being confident of this, that he who began a good work in you will carry it on to completion until the day of Christ Jesus' (NIV). Later, when I studied theology and learnt New Testament Greek, I discovered that the passage is in fact ambiguous. The Greek speaks of completing the work *en humin*, which is in the plural. It could be translated 'in you all' or corporately 'among you'. To my surprise (and disappointment), I was not the first to have spotted this. Ralph Martin, in his 1959 IVP commentary, says that the verse 'reveals Paul's unshakable confidence that the community at Philippi will be preserved in spite of its sufferings'.[2] It is probably not an individual promise and the NRSV (1989) renders it 'the one who began a good work among you'.

This prompted me to search out other occurrences of this phrase.

The great hymn to Jesus in Philippians 2:6–11 is introduced with the words 'Your attitude should be the same as that of Christ Jesus' (NIV), which sounds very individual. Each of us is to emulate Jesus' great example of humility. However, this rendering manages to obscure the fact that, once again, the Greek phrase *en humin* is present. This is brought out by NRSV ('Let the same mind be in you that was in Christ Jesus'), though on this occasion, it is content to leave the 'in you' ambiguous. The RSV was clear that it is corporate ('Have this mind among yourselves'). Once again, I wondered whether this was an original insight on my part but Martin had got there first: 'Thus *in you* does not imply the inculcation of personal virtue based on a moral example, but means "in your church fellowship", so sorely harassed by strife and plagued by arrogance.'[3]

A third example is in Philippians 2:12–13. It is doubtful if you could get a more individual sounding pair of verses: 'Therefore, my beloved, just as you have always obeyed me, not only in my presence, but much more now in my absence, work out your own salvation with fear and trembling; for it is God who is at work in you, enabling you both to will and to work for his good pleasure.' My first reaction to this passage was that this is a peculiar thing to write in a letter that continually exhorts them to consider the interests of others rather than their own (e.g. 1:27; 2:2–4). It is this attitude of thinking only of themselves that is causing the disunity. However, once again the 'in you' corresponds to the Greek *en humin* and so the clause could be rendered 'for it is God who is at work among you', which would fit with the previous two examples. But what of the phrase 'work out your own salvation'? Surely that is crystal clear? I turned to Martin and he did not disappoint:

> The situation of discord and fearfulness at Philippi controls the exegesis of the present verse... true exegesis must begin with a definition of *salvation*, not in personal terms, but in regard to the corporate life of the Philippian church. The readers are being encouraged to concentrate upon reforming their church life, 'working at' (Moffatt) this matter until the spiritual health of the community, diseased by strife and bad feeling, is restored.[4]

Martin was not working with 'liberation' principles. He simply believed that the context of these verses in Philippians makes an individual interpretation unlikely. But what I found challenging was to see how much my interpretations of Scripture were coloured by what I had been told was its main message. Once freed of that presupposition, texts took on all sorts of new meanings. Liberation theology suggests that such choices are by no means neutral or arbitrary. People naturally adopt positions that support their own well-being and security. To take to heart the 'fact' that Jesus had far more to say about poverty and injustice than he did about individuals receiving salvation is an uncomfortable one for Christians living in relative affluence. Great evangelistic campaigns portray the Church as having a mission to the world. Liberation theology suggests that we who support an economic system that keeps third world countries in debt are part of the problem rather than the solution. And if we wonder why it is that many in the West are not interested in committing their lives to Christ, we might ask ourselves why it is that so few Christians are willing to sell their possessions and give to the poor. It suits us to focus on a spiritual gospel!

Feminist readings

Feminist theologians insist that women's experience is different from that of men. This judgement is not based on agreed psychological differences (all men are like this... all women are like that...), which are too simplistic. Rather, it is based on the fact that society has been largely organized around male dominance and men and women have inevitably experienced this in different ways. On the analogy of liberation theology, it has seemed self-evident to many men that God should be called Father, King, Lord, Master, for that is what *He* is. Attempts to call God 'Mother' or use 'inclusive' language in church services ('people' instead of 'men') have met with resistance because they challenge the *status quo*. Rosemary Radford Ruether (*Sexism and God-Talk: Towards a Feminist Theology*, 1983) says:

> The critical principle of feminist theology is the promotion of the full humanity of woman. Whatever denies, diminishes, or distorts the full humanity of women is, therefore, appraised as not redemptive.[5]

There is no one set of opinions that we can call feminist theology. Each writer is seeking to do justice to 'women's experience' but how they go about it varies enormously. Some are concerned with retrieval, the bringing to light of neglected passages or themes. Others are concerned with reinterpretation, freeing the text from the bias of male interpreters down the ages. Lastly, some see no other option than rejection. Certain stories or statements in the Bible are so immersed in a patriarchal framework that they can neither be retrieved nor reinterpreted. In the name of justice, they must be rejected (as Paul rejected circumcision, even though it was commanded by God).

Retrieving the women of the Bible

In 1 Corinthians 15:3–8, Paul declares that Jesus died, was buried and was raised on the third day. His proof of the latter is that he was seen by a series of witnesses, the first of which was Peter. Then follow the other disciples, a large crowd and finally Paul himself. However, according to the resurrection stories in John (20:16) and Matthew (28:9), it is Mary Magdalene who is the first to see Jesus. While the male disciples have all fled, the women stay with Jesus at the cross and thus see where he is buried. They are then favoured with the first resurrection appearance. Opinions differ as to why Paul omits to mention this. Possibly the testimony of a woman would not have been acceptable and so a man is mentioned first. Possibly it was important for early Christianity to accord this honour to Peter ('the rock', according to Matt 16:18). Whatever the reason, a man is exalted at the expense of a woman. Imagine how the history of Christianity might have been different if the New Testament was unanimous that the Church was founded on the testimony of Mary Magdalene!

Retrieving feminine images of God

The Bible uses both feminine and masculine images to express God's character but only the masculine ones have found their way into the Church's doctrine and liturgy. God is referred to as 'He'. 'He' has revealed himself in his 'Son'. Even the Spirit, which is a feminine word in Hebrew (*ruach*), is referred to as 'He'. But there are other images. Isaiah 66:13 says: 'As a mother comforts her child, so I will comfort you; you shall be comforted in Jerusalem.' The image of childbirth is used of God bringing His (?) people into being. Jesus says: 'How often have I desired to gather your children together as a hen gathers her brood under her wings, and you were not willing!' (Matt 23:37). Wisdom is personified in the Old Testament as God's co-worker from the very beginning:

> The Lord created me at the beginning of his work,
> the first of his acts of long ago.
> Ages ago I was set up, at the first, before the beginning of the earth.
> When there were no depths I was brought forth,
> when there were no springs abounding with water.
> Before the mountains had been shaped, before the hills,
> I was brought forth... (Prov 8:22–25)

Wisdom was feminine. The first verse of Proverbs 8 begins: 'Does not wisdom call, and does not understanding raise *her* voice?' The idea of Wisdom being God's co-worker in creation was taken up in the New Testament as a way of expressing Jesus' role ('He is the image of the invisible God, the firstborn of all creation; for in him all things in heaven and on earth were created' – Col 1:15–16). Yet the feminine imagery has been lost. We have already mentioned that the Hebrew word for Spirit is feminine. The Greek translation, *pneuma,* is neuter but it is usually translated by masculine pronouns when the Holy Spirit is meant. It is only the Latin *spiritus* that is masculine from a grammatical point of view and this has been hugely important in the development of liturgy. Nevertheless, some modern liturgies are trying to retrieve the feminine imagery:

> The blessing of the God of Sarah and Abraham,
> the blessing of the Son who was born of Mary,
> the blessing of the Holy Spirit,
> who watches over us like a mother over her children, be with us all.
> Amen.[6]

Reinterpreting biblical stories

As well as retrieving stories that honour women (that male interpreters have neglected), feminist studies have brought new perspectives to familiar stories. For example, prohibition about women's dress in the New Testament (1 Cor 11:6; 1 Pet 3:3–4) is usually taken as a 'woman's problem'. But considering that it is men who wrote these letters, is it not more likely that it was the men who were having the problems? Christianity gave a new freedom to women. They could participate in worship, could prophesy, evangelize etc. This inevitably led to issues about spirituality and sexuality in the congregation and the way that the male authors appear to have dealt with it (and have done ever since) was to make it a woman's problem. If men are finding 'attraction' a problem then it is the woman who must 'cover up' or 'withdraw' or 'be quiet'.

Reclaiming biblical stories for women is sometimes called *depatriarchalization.* It openly recognizes that most (if not all) of the biblical stories are written by men and therefore carry with them a patriarchal bias. These can only be 'good news' for women if they are reinterpreted in the light of modern perceptions. An analogy may help. When we consider the problems that affect us today (nuclear war, overpopulation, global pollution, embryo research, AIDS), we find that the Bible has very little to say directly, since such issues were not envisaged at the time. Some will conclude from this that the Bible is irrelevant to modern life (and some feminists have done so). Others will try and discern principles from the Bible that can be applied today, such as being made in God's image or God's concern for justice. In his day, Paul accepted that women could play a part in ministry (Phil 4:3; Rom 16:1) but seems to have had a greater concern that the new Church did not cause offence and hence hinder the spread of the gospel. He therefore imposed restrictions. He claimed that in the gospel there was no longer 'male or female' but his practice does not always reflect this. We can reasonably ask whether he would give the same advice today, given society's (growing) acceptance of the principle of equal rights.

The woman at the well (John 4:4–42)

This well-known story has been the subject of several recent studies. The 'traditional' reading sees Jesus (the male) in conversation with the Samaritan (the female) but operating on a different (higher) plane. Her mind is set on earthly matters. She has come to the well for ordinary water (7). When Jesus speaks of 'living water', all she can think of is 'Sir, you have no bucket'. When he explains that 'Everyone who drinks of this water will be thirsty again, but those who drink of the water that I will give them will never be thirsty', her interest is aroused but only to save herself the daily journey (15). When Jesus exposes the fact that she has had five husbands (16), she tries to embroil him in a theological discussion about places of worship. But, once again, Jesus is on a higher plane. Worship is not about place but spirit and truth (24). Lastly, she voices a basic tenet of her Samaritan beliefs: 'I know that Messiah is coming... When he comes, he will proclaim all things to us' (25). Jesus replies 'I am he, the one who is speaking to you' (26).

Sandra Schneiders (*The Revelatory Text*, 1991) calls this the typical male reading of the story which 'presents the woman as a disreputable (if interesting) miscreant who, failing in her attempt to distract Jesus from her sexually disgraceful past, surrenders to his overpowering preternatural knowledge of her, alerts her fellow townspeople to his presence, and then fades from the scene as they discover for themselves and come to believe in him'.[7] But a different reading is possible, for it is Jesus who asks for a drink. It is not that the woman can only think in earthly terms; this is what Jesus asks for. He is sitting by Jacob's great well and asks her for a (material) drink. But the woman looks beyond the material to ask why social taboos are being ignored, for 'Jews do not share things in common with Samaritans'. Jesus replies that he can offer 'living water', which the woman (rightly) takes as a religious claim to be superior to Jacob and the patriarchs. Jesus then elaborates that the water he offers is such that those who drink of it will never again be thirsty for it 'will become in them a spring of water gushing up to eternal life'. The woman is interested and replies using the same metaphor as Jesus used: 'Sir, give me this water, so that I may never be thirsty or have to keep coming here to draw water.' Thus it is possible to read the text as a serious theological exchange and not a (foolish) woman continually misunderstanding the (superior) male. On this reading, she is far more astute than Nicodemus in the previous episode (3:1–21) and the disciples in this one (4:27).

Challenging biblical stories which support patriarchy

Consider the 'household code' in Ephesians 5 (paralleled in Col 3). The injunction given in 5:21 appears to be the main principle: 'Be subject to one another out of reverence for Christ.' It is found in other letters. For example, Philippians 2:4 says 'Let each of you look not to your own interests, but to the interests of others'. It envisages a mutuality between people in the body of Christ. We are not to stand on our rights but to work for the common good. Each person is made in the image of God and is worthy of respect. However, in terms of maintaining order, it appears that the author of Ephesians can only imagine this happening if someone is 'the boss':

5:22 Wives, be subject to your husbands...
6:1   Children, obey your parents...
6:5   Slaves, obey your earthly masters...

Even apart from the mental and physical abuse that has been done in the name of these commands, we would have to ask today whether such rigid hierarchical relationships are really the way to a healthy society. Partners who discuss, communicate and agree on decisions are far more likely to build a wholesome relationship than are those whose relationship is based on the dominance of one party (male or female). We know that such power relationships existed in the surrounding society but, as we shall see below, this was not how it should be among Jesus' disciples. Indeed, the pattern of his own life was 'not to be served but to serve, and to give his life a ransom for many'. Rosemary Radford Ruether says:

> Feminism appropriates the prophetic principles in ways the Biblical writers for the most part do not appropriate them, namely to criticize this unexamined patriarchal framework. Feminist theology that draws on Biblical principles is possible only if the prophetic principles, more fully understood, imply a rejection of every elevation of one social group against others as image and agent of God, every use of God to justify social domination and subjugation.

Patriarchy itself must fall under the Biblical denunciation of idolatry and blasphemy, the idolizing of the male as representative of divinity. It is idolatrous to make males more 'like God' than females.[8]

Whatever the function of such biblical stories or statements in the past, if they promote or otherwise authorize the subjugation of woman, they cannot be God's will: 'Theologically speaking, whatever diminishes or denies the full humanity of women must be presumed not to reflect the divine.'[9] Too often texts like Genesis 3:16 or 1 Corinthians 14:34 have been used as weapons against women. Some people might be able to persuade themselves that they can be reinterpreted; others will dismiss them in the name of justice, as Paul had to do with circumcision and the food laws. Such laws, though an integral part of the Law, meant that Jewish Christians could not eat with Gentile Christians (Gal 2), which was clearly intolerable in a community which celebrated its unity in a meal. Nevertheless, to abandon such food laws was a formidable step for they are part of Holy Scripture. And, according to Acts 21:20–21, the Christians in Jerusalem were quick to point this out to Paul: 'You see, brother, how many thousands of believers there are among the Jews, and they are all zealous for the law. They have been told about you that you teach all the Jews living among the Gentiles to forsake Moses, and that you tell them not to circumcise their children or observe the customs.' Unfortunately, Acts does not record Paul's answer but, in his letters to Galatians and Romans, he argues that such laws must not stand in the way of God's purpose to create 'one body in Christ'. In doing so, Paul employs the prophetic principle of using one part of Scripture to interpret (in this case, set aside) another.

Elisabeth Schüssler Fiorenza (*In Memory of Her: A Feminist Theological Reconstruction of Christian Origins*, 1994) adopts a more historical approach. She maintains that the evidence of the Gospels suggests that the 'Jesus movement' was originally an egalitarian group of men and women. Jesus taught them to turn their backs on the hierarchical structures and power-seeking of the world. The kingdom was not to be like this. They were to treat one another as equals. They were not to seek power over one another or force people into submissive roles. She illustrates this by citing Jesus' response to two 'male-orientated' questions:

Mark 10:2 'Is it lawful for a man to divorce his wife?'
Mark 12:23 'In the resurrection whose wife will she be? For the seven had married her.'

In the first question, Jesus is being asked to enter the rabbinic debate about the grounds for divorce. Should it be only for infidelity or for a variety of lesser reasons (like burning the dinner)? However, Jesus overturns this patriarchal concept of marriage by declaring that divorce was only permitted 'because of your hardness of heart' (Mark 10:5). God created male and female people and marriage is about male and female people becoming 'one flesh' (quoting the Genesis story). The idea of one partner (male or female) being able to dispose of the other is against God's will.

In the second question, a rather bizarre story is concocted about a woman marrying a succession of brothers in order to ridicule belief in the resurrection (since it was assumed that she would be married to all of them in the afterlife). But, once again, Jesus denies their patriarchal concept of marriage, whereby a woman's function is simply to continue the (male) line. In the afterlife, people 'neither marry nor are given in marriage, but are like angels in heaven' (Mark 12:25).

Schüssler Fiorenza claims that these two examples show that Jesus refused to accept a patriarchal concept of marriage that makes one partner subordinate to the other. Furthermore, he did this by referring to both God's intention from the beginning and the life to which we are moving (heaven). A marriage ceremony does not exempt a husband from Jesus' basic principle of discipleship:

> You know that among the Gentiles those whom they recognize as their rulers lord it over them, and their great ones are tyrants over them. But it is not so among you; but whoever wishes to become great among you must be your servant, and whoever wishes to be first among you must be slave of all. (Mark 10:42b–44)

Clearly this is more than an appeal to 'women's experience'. Schüssler Fiorenza is using historical criticism to get at what the original 'Jesus movement' was like, before it became overlaid with patriarchal assumptions. Other feminist scholars believe that Jesus is not quite as exempt from patriarchal bias as Schüssler Fiorenza claims and that she is basically finding what she wants to find. Nevertheless, the relationship between Jesus and women in the Gospels has been an important factor in undermining patriarchal assumptions.

The significance of the canon

Historical study has often been guilty of exclusively focusing on something behind the text, such as a particular reconstruction of its composition. Literary criticism focuses on the text in front of us but as a self-contained entity. Differences between the Gospels are deliberately shut out so as to focus on the story-world of the particular

Gospel. But that is not how the biblical books have functioned in the Christian Church. We do have four Gospels and, for at least 1,800 years, each has been read in the light of the others. Brevard Childs suggests that the meaning of a text is not to be located in its original context or what it might mean to specific interest groups today. The meaning of a text (for the Christian) lies in its role and function in the canon of Scripture. It is only thus that any particular text is 'the word of God'.

Childs does not deny the value of historical and literary approaches to the text. Clarifying the particular emphases of each biblical book has brought out the richness of the biblical witness. But the part is not the whole. The Church in its wisdom (and inspiration) canonized four Gospels, two accounts of Israel's history (Kings and Chronicles), collections of prophecies, proverbs and psalms, and various books that we now know to be composite. For the Christian, this is the context of interpretation. It is not what lies behind the text (which remains hypothetical) nor what a particular interest group or ideology decides. The text must be seen as part of the total witness of Scripture.

As an example, chapter 16 of Childs' book *Old Testament Theology in a Canonical Context* (1985) considers 'Male and female as a theological problem'. He acknowledges that Genesis 1 and Genesis 2 – 3 come from different sources. The first is from the priestly writer where no 'differentiation is made between male and female in terms of temporal priority or function. Their creation occurs simultaneously and only together is their creative role described.'[10] The second account is from a different source and Childs recognizes that it has been used to justify all sorts of male domination: 'To speak of the creation of the woman as an afterthought is certainly to do an injustice to the sense of the chapter... The creation of woman, which is sequential in time, forms a climax to the creation which resounds with joy at the close of the chapter.'[11] Nevertheless, Childs is clear that the 'woman is assigned a function as helper which is not identical with the role of the one being helped'.[12] What then is the canonical significance of these two accounts standing side by side in Holy Scripture? Primarily, says Childs, in the way that they refute two types of error:

> On the one hand, the danger from the theological right is to read into the Old Testament the traditional ideology of a male dominated society which would transfer the *mores* of a fallen society to the kingdom of God. To them the answer is No. 'Male and female created he them.' Together in their unity they constitute true human-ity. On the other hand, the danger from the theological left is to equate the biblical witness with a modern egalitarian ideology which would simply identify the sexes in every respect with the same roles,

goals, and capacities. To them the answer is likewise No. 'It is not good that the man should be alone. I will make for him a helper... therefore, a man leaves his father and mother and cleaves to his wife...' God chose to create two different forms of humanity for different functions within his creation.[13]

Childs is making an important point about the context of interpretation. Literary studies insist that the focus of attention should be the final text, rather than a reconstruction of its sources. And there has been great benefit in reading Mark's Gospel (for example) on its own terms. Childs takes this further. It was not just the sources that were given a new context when incorporated into the various books. The books themselves were given a new context when they were collected together to form the canon of Scripture. Thus while it is possible to read John's Gospel in a way that denies the humanity of Christ (as the Gnostics did), this is not an option for those who view it as belonging to the canon of Scripture. The literary technique of 'let's read it as if we were reading it for the very first time' is naïve. None of us is in that situation for very long.

On the other hand, his approach has a number of drawbacks. For example, it undoubtedly moves in the direction of harmonization. Difficult texts are brought into line with the majority view and hence lose their ability to challenge or shock. When one has read feminist critiques of patriarchy, his comments about Genesis seem conservative in the extreme. His canonical approach offers a valuable criticism to obsessive historical reconstruction and piecemeal literary analysis but seems to rule out a genuinely prophetic function for Scripture. Furthermore, in treating the canon of Scripture as the basic unit of study, authorial intention is projected onto God ('God chose to create two different forms of humanity for different functions'). At least redaction critics only claimed to know the mind of the individual authors!

Conclusion

One of the most significant developments in biblical studies has been the influence of the reader in the interpretative process. The Enlightenment ideal of detachment and neutrality is simply not possible. Where we stand affects what we see and this is why there is such diversity of opinion among biblical scholars. Even the view that Mark is the earliest Gospel is disputed by some (e.g. W. R. Farmer, *The Synoptic Problem*, 1964). Liberation and feminist theologians exploit this by declaring their own interests and challenging the hidden interests of others. Childs claims that the proper context for interpretation is not the original intention of the authors but the role the book now has as part of the canon of Scripture (though not all churches operate with the same canon). We will pursue this further in Chapter 7, when we consider 'The Bible in a postmodern world'. Before that, we must deal with an issue that we have so far kept in the background. How can we call the Bible 'the word of God' when the various versions of the Bible differ from one another?

FURTHER READING

As well as the books mentioned in this chapter, see the two works by P. Trible, *God and the Rhetoric of Sexuality* (Fortress Press, 1978/SCM, 1992) and *Texts of Terror: Literary-Feminist Readings of Biblical Narratives* (Fortress Press, 1984). C. Rowland and M. Corner, *Liberating Exegesis: The Challenge of Liberation Theology to Biblical Studies* (John Knox Press/SPCK, 1990) offer a more general approach, while a conference at King's College, London in 1992 resulted in an excellent book, edited by Francis Watson, *The Open Text: New Directions for Biblical Studies?* (SCM, 1993).

NOTES

1. J. Moltmann, *The Crucified God* (SCM, 1974), p. 201.
2. R. P. Martin, *The Epistle of Paul to the Philippians* (Inter-Varsity Press, 1959), p. 62.
3. Ibid., p. 95.
4. Ibid., pp. 110–11.
5. R. Radford Ruether, *Sexism and God-Talk: Towards a Feminist Theology* (SCM, 1983), pp. 18–19.
6. Taken from a World Council of Churches service book, quoted in M. Bührig, *Woman Invisible: A Personal Odyssey in Christian Feminism* (Burns & Oates, 1993), p. 62.
7. S. M. Schneiders, *The Revelatory Text: Interpreting the New Testament as Sacred Scripture* (HarperCollins, 1991), p. 194.
8. *Sexism and God-Talk*, p. 23.
9. Ibid., p. 19.
10. B. Childs, *Old Testament Theology in a Canonical Context* (SCM, 1985), p. 189.
11. Ibid., p. 191.
12 Ibid.
13 Ibid. p. 192.

6

Which version of the Bible is the word of God?

I have often been in Bible studies when someone says that a particular phrase means a lot to them – only to have someone else say 'My version doesn't say that'. In a modern version of the Bible, Mark's Gospel ends with the story of the empty tomb and the women running away in fear (Mark 16:8). In the King James Version, the story continues for another dozen verses, telling of resurrection appearances and a great commission (a rather odd one with the promise that snake-bites will have no effect on them). Similarly, the much-loved story of the woman caught in adultery (John 7:53 – 8:11) is printed as a separate paragraph in modern editions because it is no longer thought to be part of the original text. If Christians want to claim that the Bible is the 'word of God', which version do they have in mind?

In our diagram of the horizontal and vertical axis of biblical interpretation, we have been naïvely assuming that the text in front of us is the same as that which left the hands of the author or editor. But this is not the case. We have at best copies of copies and, in many cases, copies of copies of copies of copies. So where should we place God in our diagram? Does inspiration affect only the original so that no one today can claim to possess the 'word of God'? Or does it also apply to the transmission of the Bible, so that what we have in front of us is 'good enough'? And what about the countless millions who have felt God speak to them through the story of the 'woman caught in adultery'? Were they mistaken? Or does God, in his grace, speak through a text that is imperfect, just as He speaks and works through human beings who are imperfect?

The transmission of the Bible

Though texts were copied with great care in the ancient world, it was inevitable (human) that errors would creep in. Thus words were sometimes omitted or mistaken for other words. There was no punctuation in the original texts and so it was not always clear where one word ended and another began. Whole lines were sometimes omitted if the first word on the line was the same as that of the previous line. And sometimes the state of the text was such that a word was unreadable or had been crossed out. Despite their commitment to accuracy, those who copied manuscripts for a living had a formidable task.

Now if omissions were the only type of errors, restoring the text would be relatively easy. One would simply need to locate the manuscript with the fullest text. However, the complexity of the surviving manuscripts suggests that when the next generation of copyists found a sentence with a word or phrase missing, they tried to fill in what they thought it must have been. Some, no doubt, got it right but many got it wrong. And these errors were then copied as part of the original text, as well as introducing errors of their own. The result is that, apart from those fragments that only contain a few words, we now possess over five thousand Greek manuscripts of the New Testament, no two of which are identical. The Bible that you have in your hand is a result of editorial judgement. And this can sometimes be very significant. Consider, for example, Luke's version of the Gethsemane story as printed in the RSV (1971, 2nd edition) and the slightly later NIV (1978):

Luke 22:40–46 (RSV 2nd edn)	*Luke 22:40–46 (NIV)*
And when he came to the place he said to them,	On reaching the place, he said to them,
'Pray that you may not enter into temptation.'	'Pray that you will not fall into temptation.'
And he withdrew from them about a stone's throw, and knelt down and prayed,	He withdrew about a stone's throw beyond them, knelt down and prayed,
'Father, if thou art willing, remove this cup from me; nevertheless not my will, but thine, be done.'	'Father, if you are willing, take this cup from me; yet not my will, but yours be done.'
	An angel from heaven appeared to him and strengthened him.
	And being in anguish, he prayed more earnestly, and his sweat was like drops of blood falling to the ground.
And when he rose from prayer, he came to the disciples and found them sleeping for sorrow,	When he rose from prayer and went back to the disciples, he found them asleep, exhausted from sorrow.
and he said to them, 'Why do you sleep? Rise and pray that you may not enter into temptation.'	'Why are you sleeping?' he asked them. 'Get up and pray so that you will not fall into temptation.'

Reading the story from the RSV (2nd edition), there is little to suggest that this was a great ordeal for Jesus. In fact the point of the story seems to be more about providing the disciples with an illustration of 'lead us not into temptation'. Jesus asks that the cup might be taken from him but is only concerned to do God's will. Having prayed, he gets up, reminds the disciples of the need for prayer, and accepts his arrest. The next verse reads: 'While he was still speaking, there came a crowd, and the man called Judas, one of the twelve, was leading them. He drew near to Jesus to kiss him' (22:47). However, the NIV prints two extra verses in between Jesus' request and his return to the disciples. The effect is dramatic. Far from simply accepting his fate, Jesus now wrestles in prayer to such an extent that he needs an angel to strengthen his resolve. His sweat is like 'drops of blood falling to the ground'. He is in anguish (the Greek word is *agōnia*). Thus our understanding of this episode clearly depends on which version of the Bible we are reading. Do the extra verses come from Luke or were they added by a later copyist?

Redaction criticism would tend to suggest that it is not the sort of addition that Luke would make to Mark. As we have seen with the crucifixion, Luke changes the emphasis from despair to one of heroic acceptance. And he appears to have done the same with Mark's introduction to the Gethsemane story. Mark's comment that Jesus 'began to be distressed and agitated' has disappeared. Jesus' own words that he was 'deeply grieved, even to death' have also gone and instead of 'threw himself on the ground', we have the more devout 'knelt down and prayed'. In fact, he does not even mention the name Gethsemane:

Mark 14:32–34 (NRSV)	*Luke 22:40–41 (NRSV)*
They went to a place called Gethsemane; and he said to his disciples, 'Sit here while I pray.' He took with him Peter and James and John, *and began to be distressed and agitated.* And said to them, '*I am deeply grieved, even to death*; remain here, and keep awake.' And going a little farther, he *threw himself on the ground*...	When he reached the place, he said to them, 'Pray that you may not come into the time of trial.' Then he withdrew from them about a stone's throw, knelt down, and prayed...

However, this needs to be balanced by the probability or otherwise of a later copyist adding the words and subsequent copyists treating them as original. If this is the case, it must have happened very early since Christians in the second century knew the reading (e.g. Justin Martyr, Irenaeus). On the other hand, it does not appear in our earliest manuscript of Luke to contain the passage (Bodmer papyrus, early third century) or our earliest codex (Vaticanus, fourth century). Modern commentators agree that the evidence is finely balanced, with Christopher Evans (1990) and John Nolland (1993) rejecting the reading, while Charles Talbert (1982) accepts it.[1]

Another example is the manner in which Mark introduces his quotation about John the Baptist: 'See, I am sending my messenger ahead of you, who will prepare your way; the voice of one crying out in the wilderness.' The first part of the quotation comes from Malachi 3:1 (possibly combined with Exod 23:20). The second is definitely from Isaiah 40:3. Now the majority of manuscripts introduce this quotation with the words 'As it is written in the prophets', and this is printed in the King James Version. However, about a dozen manuscripts (including the two oldest) have the more specific 'As it is written in Isaiah the prophet'. What did Mark actually write? Modern translations adopt the latter because (1) it is supported by the earliest manuscripts and (2) since 'Isaiah' is not strictly correct (the next words come from Malachi), it is easy to see why later copyists would change it to 'prophets'. It is much more difficult to explain why a copyist would change a perfectly good reading ('prophets') to an awkward one ('Isaiah'). Thus modern Bibles go against the majority of manuscripts (thousands) and print 'Isaiah' (though only supported by a dozen manuscripts).

Textual critics make use of the principle 'prefer the harder reading', because it explains why later copyists introduced a change. It is much harder to understand why a perfectly good reading was changed to something obscure (with nobody noticing). However, this has to be balanced by the age of the manuscripts and the intrinsic probability of the reading. For example, in the story of the leper, most manuscripts say that Jesus was 'moved with pity' (Mark 1:41). There are a few, however, that say he was 'moved with anger'. Now this is undoubtedly the harder reading and it is easy to see why copyists would have assumed that it cannot be correct. However, unlike the 'Isaiah' reading discussed above, none of the manuscripts supporting it is early and so most modern versions regard it as spurious.

A good illustration of another sort of problem is the way the Lord's Prayer is said in our churches. Many now use the modern form which speaks of 'sins' rather than the obscure 'trespasses' and dispenses with 'thy' and 'thine'. But with informal gatherings, where there is no text in front of us, I have found that groups tend to revert to the old form or, more usually, a mixture of both. I can no longer trust myself to lead the Lord's Prayer without a text to guide me for the very same reason. I mix them up. Now according to the NRSV, Jesus gave the Lord's Prayer in two forms:

Matthew 6:9–13
Our Father in heaven,
hallowed be your name.
Your kingdom come.
Your will be done,
on earth as it is in heaven.
Give us this day our daily bread.
And forgive us our debts,
as we also have forgiven our debtors.

And do not bring us to the time of trial,
but rescue us from the evil one.

Luke 11:2–4
Father,
hallowed be your name.
Your kingdom come.

Give us each day our daily bread.
And forgive us our sins,
for we ourselves forgive everyone
indebted to us.
And do not bring us to the time of trial.

Now if ever there was a passage of Scripture which one would expect to be transmitted accurately, it would be this. Jesus is teaching his disciples and says to them 'When you pray, say'. And yet, if our modern versions of the Bible are correct, Luke's version is considerably shorter than Matthew's. And neither has the familiar ending: 'For thine is the kingdom, the power, and the glory, for ever and ever. Amen.' The usual explanation for this is that when each Evangelist got to the point where they wanted to include the Lord's Prayer (the settings are different), they included it in the form that was being used in their own churches. Consciously or unconsciously, they replaced oral tradition with the form that was familiar to them. But this was problematic for later copyists who assumed that they must have been the same. The net result was that the majority of later manuscripts have virtually the same prayer in both Matthew and Luke, with Matthew also gaining a liturgical ending (probably from 1 Chron 29:11–13). Thus the King James Version reads:

Matthew 6:9–13 (KJV)
Our Father which art in heaven,
Hallowed be thy name.
Thy kingdom come.
Thy will be done in earth,
as it is in heaven.
Give us this day our daily bread.
And forgive us our debts,
as we forgive our debtors.

And lead us not into temptation,
but deliver us from evil:
For thine is the kingdom, and the
power, and the glory, for ever. Amen.

Luke 11:2–4 (KJV)
Our Father which art in heaven,
Hallowed be thy name.
Thy kingdom come.
Thy will be done,
as in heaven, so in earth,
Give us day by day our daily bread.
And forgive us our sins;
for we also forgive every one that is
indebted to us.
And lead us not into temptation;
but deliver us from evil.

Modern versions of the Bible

Modern versions of the Bible differ in several ways. The first, as we have seen, is that they make different choices about what the original text *said*. The second factor is that translations make different choices about what the original *meant*. For example, there is a difficult passage in 1 Thessalonians 4:4, where the moral exhortation is to '*ktasthai* one's own vessel in holiness and honour'. The ordinary meaning of *ktasthai* is 'take' (Matt 10:9: 'Take no gold') or 'obtain' (Acts 8:20: 'obtain God's gift with money'). Thus KJV renders 'every one of you should know how to possess his vessel in sanctification and honour', which is literal but incomprehensible. The RSV takes 'vessel' to mean 'wife' (the next verse is about lust!) and renders 'each one of you know how to take a wife for himself'. In some Greek writings, 'vessel' is used in a crude phallic sense, which would fit well with the passage if *ktasthai* could be rendered 'control'. NEB does not wish to be crude but follows this line of thought with its 'each one of you must learn to gain mastery over his body' (similarly NRSV and NIV, which use the word 'control'). Perhaps surprisingly, the Good News Bible has the rather tame 'Each of you men should know how to live with his wife', while the Jerusalem Bible has 'each one of you to know how to use the body that belongs to him', which is ambiguous. Does it mean his own body or his wife's?

Thirdly, different versions of the Bible have different translation policies. For example, the GNB seeks to avoid technical language like 'righteousness', which is rare in ordinary usage (the exception being the phrase 'self-righteous'). It therefore uses expressions like 'to do what God requires' (Matt 5:6). Unfortunately, this means losing the rich background of the word 'righteousness'. Rather different is the question of inclusive language. When Paul addresses a congregation with the word 'brothers' (*adelphoi*), was he referring to everyone or just the men? Almost all scholars would say that he was addressing everyone, in the way that 'mankind' has been used to mean everyone. Thus a number of translations now speak of 'brothers and sisters', not as an attempt to be 'politically correct' but as an attempt to get closer to what Paul actually meant. As it says on the inside cover of the NIV (Inclusive Language Edition, 1995): 'Where the original languages are considered to refer to humanity in general or to a person of either gender but do so using masculine terminology, revisions have been made to restore the intention of the original texts.' However, it refuses to consider whether the gender-specific language used for God (i.e. male) requires revision: 'God's own self-descriptions in the Bible are masculine and are translated as such.'

Conclusion

It is sometimes a fundamentalist argument that though people differ in their interpretations of the Bible, the word itself is from God and therefore infallible (God would not lie or make mistakes). We have already noted that this places all the emphasis on the 'divine' side and does not take seriously the 'human' aspect of the writings. Thus Jesus can contrast what Moses wrote about divorce with God's intention for marriage (Mark 10:2–9) and Paul can decide that certain aspects of God's Law are no longer in force. However, whether such a claim is true or not, the simple fact is that we do not have the original texts anyway. We have a multitude of manuscripts, all of which differ in some way or another. Textual critics seek to determine what the original is most likely to have been, given the variations found in the manuscript tradition. But it is not an exact science. Opinions of what a scribe is likely to have done or what Luke is likely to have written are all part of the equation.

Interpretation then is unavoidable. There is no such thing as absolute objectivity or a completely neutral stance towards the Bible. Even the text you are using is a product of an editorial committee that has voted on which reading is thought to be original. For some, this will come as a disappointment. If we cannot be sure we are reading exactly what the original author said, why bother with the Bible at all? But you might as well say that unless there exists a perfect church, I am not going to join it. Or unless I can completely know God, I am not interested in a relationship with Him. Limitation and incompleteness are integral to the human condition. But that does not mean that real insight or revelation is impossible. We just have to learn to appreciate it for what it is and not pretend that we have the whole picture. Only God has that!

FURTHER READING

For a good summary of 'Texts and Versions', see ch. 68 of the *New Jerome Biblical Commentary*. The standard work on the New Testament is B. M. Metzger, *The Text of the New Testament: Its Transmission, Corruption, and Restoration* (revised edn; OUP, 1968). A somewhat easier introduction is provided by the slim volume by K. Elliott and I. Moir, *Manuscripts and the Text of the New Testament: An Introduction for English Readers* (T. & T. Clark, 1995). For the Old Testament, see E. Würthwein, *The Text of the Old Testament* (Eerdmans/SCM, 1979).

NOTE

1. C. F. Evans, *Saint Luke* (SCM, 1990), p. 812; J. Nolland, *Luke 18:35 – 24:53* (WBC 35c; Word Books, 1993), p. 1080; C. H. Talbert, *Reading Luke* (SPCK, 1982), p. 214.

7

The Bible in a postmodern world

In our second chapter, we saw how the Enlightenment emphasis on objectivity and method led to the development of historical criticism in biblical studies. Initially, this upset many Christians because it challenged cherished beliefs, but many were eventually won over. The differences between the Gospels are real and do require some sort of explanation. Historical context seemed to provide it. The different Gospel writers were aiming to meet different needs and therefore told the story of Jesus in different ways. And if we want to evaluate the truth-claims that they make, then understanding why the Gospel writers wrote is as important as understanding what they wrote. Recognizing that Genesis contains not one but two accounts of creation changed our understanding of the purpose of these early chapters. They were not intending to give a scientific account of our origins but to make a number of theological points about God, our world and humanity.

In contrast, believing something because the Church said so was seen as indoctrination. Enlightenment people were simply unwilling to accept it. Neither was it acceptable simply to read into a text whatever meaning you wished to find. Jesus could not possibly have meant that the innkeeper in the parable was the apostle Paul. Nor could the author of Revelation have had the Pope or Adolf Hitler in mind when he wrote his book. Historical criticism aimed to bring objectivity to biblical interpretation. It aimed to produce results not just for the community of faith (who were already disposed or even required to believe them) but for any rational person who could weigh evidence and follow an argument. In short, it was believed to be a victory for truth and integrity over dogma and superstition.

But, as we saw in Chapter 4, claims to know the author's intention or how a particular text would have been received are often speculative. For most of the Old Testament, we have no idea who wrote or edited the various books, let alone something called their 'intention'. And even with those books where there is a statement of purpose (John 20:31; Luke 1:1–4), in practice this is of little help in deciding the meaning of individual passages. For example, according to John's Gospel, one of the soldiers pierced Jesus' side and 'at once blood and water came out' (John 19:34). Now there is considerable debate as to whether the aim of this reference is to show that Jesus was really dead, to show that he was human (yes, real blood!) or is a symbolic reference to Jesus giving the sacraments. Knowing that the author has written 'so that you may come to believe that Jesus is the Messiah, the Son of God' does not actually help us decide between these interpretations. We have no direct access to the mind of the author and any such talk is an illusion. A phrase like 'John intended' really means something like 'from my analysis of the text and what I consider to be its meaning, I suggest that John intended'. Put like that, it does not have quite the same ring of authority.

So attention turned to the thing that could be analysed, namely our interaction with the text in front of us. This took two forms. Some were interested in how texts affect readers. For example, how different types of narrative tend to produce (in most readers) particular responses. Or how literary devices such as irony, symbol and metaphor have an effect on how a text is read. Others felt that the key factor in interpretation was not so much the type of text but the stance of the reader. What are the psychological factors that affect our reading? Why do some people gravitate towards certain characters or plots while others ignore them? Is it simply wilfulness on our part? Or is it about protecting our own interests, as various forms of 'liberation theology' suggest?

So the last decade has seen a proliferation of studies aimed at particular interest groups. There are now feminist studies on all of the books of the Bible. There are political readings, each claiming to speak from a specific vantage point. There are readings from an ecological perspective, gay liberation and Black and Asian theologies. What is of note in all this is that each group has little (or no) confidence in studies produced by outsiders. It is only those who have shared the experience who can speak to and on behalf of the group. In short, there is now widespread scepticism that anybody can offer a universal study that is equally valid for all, rich or poor, male or female, black or white.

Furthermore, previous attempts to offer such a universal study are now seen as acts of domination. Though often cast as 'objective' or 'the author's intention' or 'the Church's teaching', each was guilty (consciously or unconsciously) of imposing its own agenda on those that differed. Clergy told lay people how to be loyal members of the Church (i.e. to be passive and do as you are told). Men told women what roles they should adopt (i.e. to be passive and do as you are told). The rich and powerful told the poor how they should live their lives (i.e. to be passive and do as you are told). And, in some cases, the penalty for nonconformity was severe. The great insight of the last decades is that 'where you stand affects what you see'. Interpretation is never neutral or objective; it is always serving somebody's interests and therefore concerns power. The key question today is: 'Who is advocating this interpretation and for what purpose?'

Postmodernism

Many people today are claiming that we now live in a postmodern world. The movement known as the Enlightenment is said to have come to an end. Modernism, with its quest for objectivity and proper method, is now seen to be an illusion. It merely veiled the particular interests of those who propagated it. In particular, it emphasized certain types of truth, such as scientific rationalism, at the expense of other forms of knowledge, such as intuition or religious experience. In the West, it has resulted in a barren secularism that measures everything in terms of its monetary value.

In part, Christians will be pleased with this challenge. Postmodernism is more open to hearing about ways of knowing that are personal and intuitive. Much of the Bible is in story form and, as we saw in Chapter 4, stories communicate by stimulating participation and imagination, not by propositional logic and rational analysis. What Genesis says about human nature is as important as what science says about our molecular composition.

Furthermore, the postmodern world is much less confident that it knows what can and cannot happen. The miracles of Jesus (and his followers) have always been a problem for people schooled in Enlightenment rationalism. Given a choice between the suspension of scientific laws and the possibility of the witnesses being mistaken, the latter has generally seemed more probable. But scientists today are much less certain about what is possible or impossible. Whether it be the power of the human mind, psychic phenomena or chaos theory, there is an increasing acknowledgement that 'fact can be stranger than fiction'.

However, there is another side to the coin. While claims to know God are more likely to gain a hearing today, they will have to take their place alongside all sorts of other claims. The view that there is somewhere a method, be it historical criticism, literary criticism or Enlightenment rationalism, that will produce truth to everyone's satisfaction has been discredited. It has too often been a device for one group to exercise power over another group. And the Church has not been exempt from this. If Christianity has something important to say to the world, then it will have to rely on its intrinsic persuasiveness rather than claims of infallibility (whether of Pope, Bible or synod).

What does this mean for biblical studies? First, it means that no one approach to the Bible has a monopoly on the truth. Historical study has an important place in biblical studies because we are dealing with historical documents. But whether historical reconstruction and hypotheses will mediate God, challenge our way of life or offer liberation to the oppressed is another question. Further, it is a sobering fact that, despite the historian's claim that a text cannot be understood apart from its context, this information is actually unavailable for most of the Old Testament. And there is certainly no guarantee that the latest scholarly reconstruction will be more 'revelatory' than those of the past.

Various forms of literary criticism invite readers to interact with the text at a deeper level. In so doing, many have become aware of new insights, renewed vision and fresh challenges. However, literary criticism can fall into the same trap as historical criticism when it claims to have discovered (for the very first time!) *the* structure of a text. The need to have complete mastery over a text appears to be the fourth temptation (or was this the devil's temptation in Matt 4:6?). And how long can the Church build on its aesthetic appreciation of biblical stories if it no longer believes in the events behind them? Literary approaches have brought many fresh insights but they also have their blind spots.

Liberation approaches are different in that they make no claim to be neutral or objective. They are quite deliberately applying an ideological slant to the interpretative process in order to serve a higher truth (such as human rights). And it has led to both positive action (laws against racism and sexism) and challenges to conventional interpretations. The weakness is that these ideological slants often have competing interests. For example, feminist studies have done much to expose the patriarchal bias of male scholars but have (so far) largely come from white, middle-class academics. From the point of view of economic liberation, they are as much a part of the problem as those coming from white, middle-class males. They share the blindness of those who are benefiting from the current social order (in economic terms). Almost by definition, liberation studies are never going to get universal assent.

What is the meaning of a text?

One of the major debating points in literary circles has been the question of whether a text possesses something called 'its meaning'. If it does, then interpretation is about finding the appropriate means of discovering it. Scholars will differ on how the evidence should be evaluated (cf. Schweitzer and Dodd) but agree that 'meaning' is there to be found. Each text possesses a single meaning, located in the author's intention or perhaps in the dynamics of the text (after all, the author might be a poor communicator). As we have seen, this was a key feature of the Enlightenment.

However, a different view is that texts always point in a number of directions, so that 'meaning' is created only when an actual reader attempts to understand it. On this view, a text can never be reduced to something called 'its meaning' but is always open to other ways of looking at it. There is no neutral access to a text. The only way of saying anything about it is to bring to it our own interests, commitments and background and see what emerges. Texts always retain the power to generate new interpretations.

Now it could be argued that this is thoroughly in line with the view expressed in Hebrews 4:12 that the 'word of God is living and active, sharper than any two-edged sword, piercing until it divides soul from spirit, joints from marrow'. To reduce it to a set of fixed meanings or doctrines is to domesticate it and ultimately rob it of its power. If texts only have one true meaning, surely scholars would have discovered it by now. On the other hand, others would argue that the doctrine of inspiration means that the true meaning of a passage is the meaning God intends. This does not necessarily make it any easier to decide what that meaning is. But it ensures that there is a stable meaning behind every text. The idea that the Bible means different things to different people seems to rule out the possibility of it exercising any authority.

Do Bible passages have a fixed meaning?

One way of pursuing this question is to look at those Old Testament texts which are quoted in the New Testament. Do they have the same meaning in the New Testament as they did in their Old Testament context? For example, consider two of the texts that occur in Matthew's birth narrative. In Matthew 1:22–23, we are told that the conception of Jesus took place 'to fulfill what had been spoken by the Lord through the prophet: "Look, the virgin shall conceive and bear a son, and they shall name him Emmanuel." ' According to Matthew, the virgin birth of Jesus was predicted in Isaiah. But if we look up Isaiah 7:14, we find that the context implies a contemporary of Isaiah:

Therefore the Lord himself will give you a sign. 'Look, the young woman is with child and shall bear a son, and shall name him

Immanuel... For before the child knows how to refuse the evil and choose the good, the land before whose two kings you are in dread will be deserted.' (Isa 7:14–16)

It is indeed a promise that the birth of a child will be a sign of deliverance. But the particular deliverance in mind is the political threat to Israel in the eighth century BCE. Before this child is weaned (i.e. very soon), the threat will have disappeared. It makes utter nonsense of Isaiah 7 to say that it refers to the birth of Jesus in seven hundred years' time. Indeed, if it does refer to Jesus, then Isaiah's contemporaries were being cruelly misled for the message would then be: 'For in seven hundred years' time, the land before whose two kings you are in dread will be deserted.' Thanks a lot!

Second, consider the flight to Egypt as recorded in Matthew 2:14–15. An angel appears to Joseph in a dream and tells him to flee to Egypt in order to escape from Herod. This is the immediate human reason for the trip. But we are also told that it happened in order to fulfil an Old Testament text:

> Now after they had left, an angel of the Lord appeared to Joseph in a dream and said, 'Get up, take the child and his mother, and flee to Egypt, and remain there until I tell you; for Herod is about to search for the child, to destroy him.' Then Joseph got up, took the child and his mother by night, and went to Egypt, and remained there until the death of Herod. This was to fulfill what had been spoken by the Lord through the prophet, 'Out of Egypt I have called my son.' (Matt 2:13–15)

The impression given by this passage is that the Old Testament predicted that God would call Jesus while he was living in Egypt. The flight to Egypt, though occasioned by the immediate need to escape from Herod, was actually a working out of God's plan. However, if we look up the text in the Old Testament, we find the following:

> When Israel was a child, I loved him, and *out of Egypt I called my son.* The more I called them, the more they went from me; they kept sacrificing to the Baals, and offering incense to idols. (Hos 11:1–2)

From this passage, the phrase 'out of Egypt I called my son' clearly refers to Israel and the Exodus. God rescued Israel out of Egypt and brought her into a close relationship (sonship). But the people were unfaithful and preferred to sacrifice to foreign gods. Thus the meaning of the phrase 'out of Egypt I called my son' is quite different in the Old Testament passage. And if anyone wishes to insist that Hosea (or God!) was referring to Jesus, then we have a problem with the next verse ('they kept sacrificing to the Baals'), for it clearly refers to the same subject. It would seem then that Matthew is giving the words of Hosea new meaning.

Indeed, the principle that the New Testament authors see the Old Testament texts in a new light is stated by Paul when he declares that 'to this very day whenever Moses is read, a veil lies over their minds; but when one turns to the Lord, the veil is removed' (2 Cor 3:15). And the various interpretations found in the New Testament confirm this. Christians inevitably interpreted texts in the light of their present experience of Christ and the Church. They did not try to imagine what the meaning would have been for the original recipients. They were interested in what the text meant to them in the light of the coming of Christ. Some have called this 'Christological' or 'Messianic' exegesis.[1] Others point to the work of the Holy Spirit. But the principle is the same. The authors of the New Testament did not ask what the texts might mean if you were ignorant of the coming of Christ, the gift of the Spirit and the birth of the Church. They tried to discern the meaning of the texts in the light of these events.

We find the same is true of the Dead Sea Scrolls. The Qumran community believed that they were living in the last days and that God's promises were being fulfilled in them. In particular, they believed that Scripture gave a detailed account of their leader ('Teacher of Righteousness') and his adversary ('Wicked Priest'). This is brought out in their commentary on the book of Habakkuk (*1QpHab*). Habakkuk's demand to hear God's voice in 2:1 ('I will keep watch to see what he will say to me, and what he will answer concerning my complaint') is answered by a rather obscure expression ('Write the vision; make it plain on tablets, so that a runner may read it'). The Qumran commentator explains:

> God told Habakkuk to write down that which would happen to the final generation, but He did not make known to him when time would come to an end. And as for that which He said, *That he who reads may read it speedily:* interpreted this concerns the Teacher of Righteousness, to whom God made known all the mysteries of the words of His servants the Prophets.[2]

On the other hand, Habakkuk's description of the proud and arrogant in 2:5 ('They open their throats wide as Sheol; like Death they never have enough') is applied to a former leader who has now become their adversary: 'Interpreted, this concerns the Wicked Priest who was called by the name of truth when he first arose. But when he ruled over Israel his heart became proud, and he forsook God and betrayed the precepts for the sake of riches.' Here then is another community which believed its history, including key figures, to be spoken about in

Scripture. If the early Church believed the Scriptures spoke about Jesus (Luke 24:44) and Judas (Matt 26:20–25), the Qumran community believed they spoke about the 'Teacher of Righteousness' and the 'Wicked Priest'. The discovery of the Dead Sea Scrolls in the latter half of the twentieth century has been of enormous importance for biblical studies.

Deconstruction

One form of postmodern biblical criticism is known as deconstruction. It attempts to expose the blind spots in conventional interpretations by showing that they are always bought at a price. For example, it now seems amazing that the Reformation view that Paul's letter to the Romans focuses on 'justification by faith alone' was not derailed by the following verses from chapter 2:

> For he will repay according to each one's deeds: to those who by patiently doing good seek for glory and honour and immortality, he will give eternal life; while for those who are self-seeking and who obey not the truth but wickedness, there will be wrath and fury. (2:6–7)

> For it is not the hearers of the law who are righteous in God's sight, but the doers of the law who will be justified. (2:13)

> So, if those who are uncircumcised keep the requirements of the law, will not their uncircumcision be regarded as circumcision? Then those who are physically uncircumcised but keep the law will condemn you that have the written code and circumcision but break the law. (2:26–27)

On any ordinary use of language, these verses seem to make the following points: (1) God rewards good people and punishes bad people; (2) goodness is determined by obedience to the Law; (3) some people do in fact obey the Law and will be justified. Now such propositions would have been anathema to the Reformation view that all stand condemned unless 'justified by faith alone'. So they must mean something else. And in order to make them mean something else, they are subject to an act of interpretative power. They are not to be taken at face value but made to conform to an overarching scheme. Thus Barrett (*The Epistle to the Romans*, 1962) explains Romans 2:6 with the words: 'The reward of eternal life, then, is promised to those who do not regard their good works as an end in themselves, but see them as marks not of human achievement but of hope in God. Their trust is not in their good works, but in God, the only source of glory, honour, and incorruption.'

However, more recent commentators recognize that such verses must be allowed a say in what Romans is all about. Paul is certainly not advocating 'salvation by works' (which he denies elsewhere) but neither is he trying to show that everyone, without exception, is desperately wicked. If that had been his purpose, he would hardly have made the above statements. Deconstruction aims to show that every attempt to 'explain' a text is always at the expense of some elements of it. It is simply impossible to reduce the complexity of a text like Romans to a single coherent purpose, intention or meaning.[3]

The woman at the well (again)

We have already looked at Schneiders' feminist interpretation of the woman at the well. She has made a strong case that this should be viewed as a serious theological discussion and not a foolish woman concerned only with earthly matters. However, it is problematic to her position that Jesus says in 4:17–18: 'You are right in saying, "I have no husband"; for you have had five husbands, and the one you have now is not your husband. What you have said is true!' Is this not confirmation that the story is about her 'sexually disgraceful past', even if male scholars have exaggerated this? Schneiders' answer is that adultery is a frequent metaphor in the Old Testament for following false gods and that this is extremely pertinent to the status of Samaritan religion. In 721 BCE, Samaria was captured by the Assyrians and re-populated with people from five foreign towns (2 Kings 17:24). Thus, according to Schneiders, Jesus is not playing games with the woman but making a serious point about her religion, which she clearly understands ('Sir, I see that you are a prophet. Our ancestors worshipped on this mountain...').

This allegorical interpretation was once quite popular though the Enlightenment has made it difficult for moderns to accept (allegory was the enemy of rationalism). However, given the symbolic nature of much of John's Gospel ('water into wine', 'footwashing', 'I am the vine'), one has to admit that it is a possibility. Stephen Moore (*Poststructuralism and the New Testament*, 1994) turns this into a 'deconstructive' point by noting that those who wish to condemn the woman for taking everything literally can do so only by insisting that 4:18 is taken literally. He says:

> They can condemn her only if they participate in her error, can ascribe a history of immorality to her only by reading as 'carnally' as she does – at which point the literal reading of 4:18 threatens to become a displaced reenactment of yet another Johannine episode,

one in which an unnamed woman is similarly charged with sexual immorality by accusers who themselves stand accused (8:1–11).[4]

Intertextuality

Another postmodern development in the theory of literature is known as intertextuality. The idea is that every text is actually a gateway to other texts. Words do not come to an author in a vacuum but from their use in previous texts (or traditions). They therefore carry with them a host of associations. For example, if I describe my home town as the 'Babylon' of south England, it evokes all sorts of images from the Bible where that term is used. Babylon was the place of exile. It was where the psalmist cried out 'How could we sing the Lord's song in a foreign land?' (Ps 137:4). It was also the place where Daniel's friends were thrown into the fiery furnace for refusing to worship Nebuchadnezzar's statue (Dan 3). Thus calling my home town 'Babylon' is not likely to be taken as a compliment. Previous associations bring connotations that are not intrinsic to the word itself (a geographical reference) but are part of its rich textual history.

This has great relevance to the New Testament since much of its writing is heavily indebted to the Old Testament. Historical criticism has shown that many of the interpretations offered by the New Testament authors could not possibly have been what the Old Testament authors meant. But this does not mean that the New Testament authors could make a text mean whatever they like. The text does not come as an isolated unit but is part of the whole tapestry of Scripture. It therefore brings with it images and connotations that continue to speak to the reader. As Richard Hays (*Echoes of Scripture in the Letters of Paul*, 1989) says: 'Echoes linger in the air and lure the reader of Paul's letters back into the symbolic world of Scripture.'[5] It is also true that much of the Old Testament is itself a reworking of older themes (see Dan 9:2), as Michael Fishbane has so convincingly shown (*Biblical Interpretation in Ancient Israel*, 1985).

Thus our previous diagram of how a reader interacts with a text is too simplistic, for every text is linked to a number of other texts. Signals come to the reader not just from one text but also from those texts to which it points. Thus, reading a passage from the New Testament, the (knowledgeable) reader often recalls a number of Old Testament texts where such words have been used before. These in turn may point to other texts, both within the canon of Scripture and outside it. In order to make sense of the New Testament passage, the reader has to configure these signals or voices into some sort of coherent meaning. But there is never just one way of doing this:

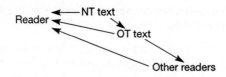

Conclusion

There is widespread agreement that the Enlightenment enterprise has run its course and that we now live in a postmodern world. But there are many ways of interpreting this. Walter Brueggemann (*The Bible and Postmodern Imagination*, 1993) believes that biblical studies today should be contextual, local and pluralistic. He explains:

> 1. Our knowing is inherently contextual... Descartes wanted to insist that context was not relevant to knowing. It is, however, now clear that what one knows and sees depends upon where one stands or sits... Contextualism argues that the knower helps constitute what is known, that the socioeconomic-political reality of the knower is decisive for knowledge.

> 2. It follows that contexts are quite *local*, and the more one generalzes, the more one loses or fails to notice context. Localism means that it is impossible to voice large truth. All one can do is to voice local truth and propose that it pertains elsewhere.

> 3. It follows from contextualism and localism that knowledge is inherently *pluralistic*, a cacophony of claims, each of which rings true to its own advocates. Indeed, pluralism is the only alternative to objectivism once the dominant center is no longer able to impose its view and to silence by force all alternative or dissenting opinion.[6]

Brueggemann is quick to point out that this does not mean that every interpretation is equally valid. Some will simply fail to convince (anyone) because they fail to do justice to the text (for anyone). Some will be so audience-specific that they are judged irrelevant by everybody else. Language is not private property. It exists in the public domain and so acts as a control on the more 'way-out' interpretations. But this does not take away from the key insight of postmodernism that every interpretation is an act of power, over people and over the text itself. Those who previously claimed to have discovered *the truth* did so at someone else's expense. Biblical studies in a postmodern world must learn to serve humanity, not dominate it. Daniel Patte (*Ethics of Biblical Interpretation*, 1995) says:

> existing critical exegeses by male European-American exegetes were originally done with the presupposition that there were two tasks to do: (1) to establish *the* (single and universally true) meaning of the text, and consequently (2) to disprove all other interpretations.[7]

In contrast, Patte believes that responsible exegesis needs to be 'multidimensional in the sense that it needs to acknowledge as equally legitimate several (rather than one) critical readings of each given text'.[8] Again, this does not mean that a text can mean whatever one likes. A theory that asserts the total relativity of everything is self-defeating, for the assertion itself would be meaningless. All enquiry takes place on the assumption that some meaningful communication takes place between human beings. But if it has any humility, it will recognize that other ways of seeing things are not only possible but very probable.

Even allegory, the enemy of Enlightenment rationalism, is finding a new lease of life. Of course Augustine was wrong if he thought that Jesus had the apostle Paul in mind when the Good Samaritan reaches the inn. But asserting a connection between the parable and the story of salvation is not as far-fetched as is often thought. Both are concerned with rescue, are motivated by compassion and show the inadequacy of contemporary religion. The phrase 'Take care of him; and when I come back, I will repay you' (Luke 10:35) is surely suggestive of Jesus' second coming, whether it was in Jesus' mind or not. As Frances Young says:

> Allegory self-consciously makes play with the inadequacies of human language for expressing the divine... Positivist views of language have impoverished theological reading of the Bible by reducing God to an item in the world of the biblical text. Allegorical reading can set free the soul for creative engagement with transcendence, and such spiritual reading with a certain open-endedness can alone do justice to the textual claim which the Bible makes.[9]

Alister McGrath (*A Passion for Truth*, 1996) offers a different assessment of postmodernism. He agrees that to 'reduce revelation to principles or concepts is to suppress the element of mystery, holiness and wonder to God's self-disclosure'.[10] Indeed, he believes that much evangelicalism needs to be freed from the negative influences of the Enlightenment:

> For understandable reasons, evangelicalism has in the past chosen to focus on the propositional or cognitive element of the complex

network of divine revelation – an element which allowed evangelicalism to maintain its credibility and integrity during a period of
rationalist assault. But the ensuing understanding of 'revelation' was
itself dangerously deficient, verging on the same aridity and sterility
which were the hallmarks of the same rationalism which evangelicalism was seeking to oppose.[11]

However, as the title of the book suggests, McGrath does not believe
this should lead to pluralism. He acknowledges that everyone comes to
the Bible with their own doctrinal framework and this affects interpretation. However, he believes that the distinctive feature of evangelical
interpretation is that its doctrinal framework is not imposed on the
Bible but arises from it:

> Doctrine thus provides the conceptual framework by which the
> scriptural narrative is interpreted. It is not an arbitrary framework,
> however, but one which is suggested by that narrative, and intimated
> (however provisionally) by scripture itself. It is to be discerned
> within, rather than imposed upon, that narrative. The narrative is
> primary, and the interpretative framework secondary.[12]

This is clearly saying something very important. Gnostics of the
second century read the Old Testament on the basis that its God was
an inferior deity. This is clearly a theoretical possibility but it is not a
Christian reading, which asserts that the God of the Old Testament is
none other than the 'Father of our Lord Jesus Christ'. The problem
comes when we consider the phrase 'however provisionally'. McGrath
seems to think that it will lead to those doctrines held dear by evangelicals and hence the subtitle of his book (*The Intellectual Coherence of
Evangelicalism*). However, most of the scholars reviewed in this book
believe that they have *discerned* something in Scripture (however
provisionally) and are now applying it more widely. For example,
feminist studies discern the principle that in Christ 'there is no longer
male and female' (Gal 3:28) but apply it in ways that Paul generally did
not.

What is clear is that scholars today are much more aware of their
own presuppositions and willing to state them. The aim of this book has
been to offer an introduction to the range of issues being debated, so
that you can enter into the discussion. If particular approaches have
caught your imagination, follow them up with some of the books
mentioned under 'Further reading'. And look out for new titles in this
series. It is an exciting time to begin a course in biblical studies. In the
past, one was often initiated into a series of historical-critical 'results'.
Today, everything is much more open. Historical studies continue to be
important as fresh evidence, such as the Dead Sea Scrolls, brings new

insights into the language of the Bible, 'types' of Judaism and parallels with the New Testament. And as we approach the year 2000, there is bound to be renewed interest in the person of Jesus. Was he an eschatological figure who thought the end was coming soon? Or is he best thought of as a Wisdom teacher or holy man? Or did the creeds get it right after all?

Literary approaches continue to provide new insights. What is it about particular stories, structures and types of language that has the power to move people? And is this changing as we move more and more into a multi-media computer culture? Will our postmodern world continue to value texts as a means of inspiration, communication and challenge? And what future is there for the world? Liberation theologies have shown us that interpretation is never neutral. Whatever one believes about inspiration, the Bible has undoubtedly been (mis)used to promote racism (notably anti-Semitism), sexism and the exploitation of the earth's resources. Responsible interpretation can no longer ignore this. There is nothing wrong with coming to the Bible with set ideas and convictions. But don't expect them to go unchallenged!

FURTHER READING

Unless you have a background in philosophy (Heidegger, Nietzsche) or literature (Derrida, Foucault), most books on postmodernism are extremely difficult. Walter Brueggemann's short book (*The Bible and Postmodern Imagination*, SCM, 1993) offers a good introduction (without the jargon) to its relevance for biblical studies. See also his *The Bible Makes Sense* (Saint Mary's Press, 1997). Another good introduction is *What Is Postmodern Biblical Criticism?* by A. K. M. Adam (Fortress Press, 1995). One form of literary criticism that we have not mentioned by name is structuralism. This aimed to protect 'meaning' from historical uncertainty by locating it in the deep structures of a text (rather like narrative and plot). But since scholars could not agree on their analyses of such structures, structuralism could not provide the objective anchor for which its proponents had hoped. Thus postmodernism is sometimes referred to as poststructuralism, as in Stephen Moore's book. See D. Patte and A. Patte, *Structural Exegeses: From Theory to Practice* (Fortress Press, 1978). For those who feel up to it, Moore's earlier book (*Literary Criticism and the Gospels: The Theoretical Challenge*, Yale University Press, 1989) shows how early experiments with reader-response criticism inevitably led to poststructuralism.

NOTES

1. D. Juel, *Messianic Exegesis: Christological Interpretations of the Old Testament in Early Christianity* (Fortress Press, 1988).
2. Text taken from G. Vermes (ed.), *The Dead Sea Scrolls in English* (3rd edn; Penguin Books, 1987).
3. See D. Seeley, *Deconstructing the New Testament* (Brill, 1994). A good discussion of the implications of this 'new view' on Romans can be found in J. D. G. Dunn, *Romans 1 – 8* (WBC 38a; Word Books, 1988).
4. S. Moore, *Poststructuralism and the New Testament* (Fortress Press, 1994), p. 49.
5. R. Hays, *Echoes of Scripture in the Letters of Paul* (Yale University Press, 1989), p. 155.
6. W. Brueggemann, *The Bible and Postmodern Imagination* (SCM, 1993), pp. 8–9.
7. D. Patte, *Ethics of Biblical Interpretation: A Reevaluation* (John Knox Press, 1995), p. 123.
8. Ibid., p. 116.
9. F. W. Young, 'Allegory and the ethics of reading' in *The Open Text*, ed. F. Watson (SCM, 1993), p. 118. An interesting comparison between readings of Scripture and musical performances is found in her *The Art of Performance* (Darton, Longman and Todd, 1990).
10. A. McGrath, *A Passion for Truth: The Intellectual Coherence of Evangelicalism* (Apollos, 1996), p. 107.
11. Ibid.
12. Ibid., p. 113.

Bibliography

Adam, A. K. M., *What Is Postmodern Biblical Criticism?* (Minneapolis: Fortress Press, 1995).

Alter, R., *The Art of Biblical Narrative* (New York: Basic Books/London: Allen and Unwin, 1981).

Alter, R. and Kermode, F. (eds), *The Literary Guide to the Bible* (Cambridge, MA: Harvard University Press/London: Collins, 1987).

Barr, J., *The Bible in the Modern World* (London: SCM/New York: Harper, 1973).

Barrett, C. K., *The Epistle to the Romans* (London: A. & C. Black, 1962).

Barton, J., *Reading the Old Testament: Method in Biblical Study* (London: Darton, Longman and Todd/Philadelphia: Westminster, 1984).

Bettenson, H. (ed.), *Documents of the Christian Church* (2nd edn; Oxford/New York: Oxford University Press, 1963).

Blomberg, C., *The Historical Reliability of the Gospels* (Leicester: Inter-Varsity Press, 1987).

Borg, M., *Jesus in Contemporary Scholarship* (Philadelphia: Trinity Press International, 1994).

Brown, R. E., *The Birth of the Messiah: A Commentary on the Infancy Narratives in Matthew and Luke* (New York: Doubleday, 1977).

Brown, R. E., *The Community of the Beloved Disciple* (London: Geoffrey Chapman, 1979).

Brueggemann, W., *The Bible and Postmodern Imagination* (London: SCM, 1993).

Brueggemann, W., *The Bible Makes Sense* (rev. edn; Winona: Saint Mary's Press, 1997).

Bührig, M., *Woman Invisible: A Personal Odyssey in Christian Feminism* (Tunbridge Wells: Burns & Oates, 1993).

Bultmann, R., *The History of the Synoptic Tradition* (Oxford: Blackwell, 1968 [1921]).

Burridge, R. A., *Four Gospels, One Jesus* (London: SPCK, 1994).

Childs, B., *The New Testament As Canon: An Introduction* (London: SCM, 1984/Philadelphia: Fortress Press, 1985).

Childs, B., *Old Testament Theology in a Canonical Context* (London: SCM/Philadelphia: Fortress Press, 1985).

Clines, D. J. A., *The Theme of the Pentateuch* (Sheffield: JSOT Press, 1978).

Conzelmann, H., *The Theology of Saint Luke* (London: Faber/New York: Harper, 1960).

Crossan, D., *The Historical Jesus: The Life of a Mediterranean Jewsih Peasant* (San Francisco: HarperCollins/Edinburgh: T. & T. Clark, 1991).

Culpepper, A., *Anatomy of the Fourth Gospel: A Study in Literary Design* (Philadelphia: Fortress Press, 1983).

Dibelius, M., *From Tradition to Gospel* (Cambridge: J. Clark, 1971).

Dodd, C. H., *The Parables of the Kingdom* (rev. edn; London: Nisbet/New York: Scribners, 1961 [1935]).

Driver, S. R., *The Book of Genesis* (Westminster Commentaries; London: Methuen, 1904).

Dunn, J. D. G., *Romans 1 – 8* (WBC 38a; Dallas: Word Books, 1988).

Elliott, K. and Moir, I., *Manuscripts and the Text of the New Testament: An Introduction for English Readers* (Edinburgh: T. & T. Clark, 1995).

Evans, C. F., *Saint Luke* (London: SCM/Philadelphia: Trinity Press International, 1990).

Farmer, W. R., *The Synoptic Problem: A Critical Analysis* (London: Macmillan, 1964).

Fishbane, M., *Biblical Interpretation in Ancient Israel* (Oxford/New York: Oxford University Press, 1985).

Fleming, D. L., *The Spiritual Exercises of Saint Ignatius: A Literal Translation and a Contemporary Reading* (St Louis: The Institute of Jesuit Resources, 1980).

Funk, R. W., Hoover, R. W. and The Jesus Seminar, *The Five Gospels: The Search for the Authentic Words of Jesus* (New York: Polebridge Press, 1993).

Gerhardsson, B., *Memory and Manuscript: Oral Tradition and Written Transmission in Rabbinic Judaism and Early Christianity* (Uppsala: Gleerup, 1961).

Goldingay, J., *Models for Scripture* (Grand Rapids: Eerdmans/Carlisle: Paternoster, 1994).

Goulder, M. D., *Luke: A New Paradigm* (Sheffield: JSOT Press, 1989).

Gundry, R., *Mark: A Commentary on His Apology for the Cross* (Grand Rapids: Eerdmans, 1993).

Gundry, R., *Matthew: A Commentary on His Handbook for a Mixed Church under Persecution* (Grand Rapids: Eerdmans, 1994).

Gunn, D., *The Story of King David* (Sheffield: JSOT Press, 1978).

Gunn, D., *The Fate of King Saul* (Sheffield: JSOT Press, 1980).

Hays, R. B., *Echoes of Scripture in the Letters of Paul* (New Haven/London: Yale University Press, 1989).

Hooker, M. D., *The Message of Mark* (London: Epworth Press, 1983).

Juel, D., *Messianic Exegesis: Christological Interpretations of the Old Testament in Early Christianity* (Philadelphia: Fortress Press, 1988).

Kermode, F., *The Genesis of Secrecy: On the Interpretation of Narrative* (Cambridge, MA: Harvard University Press, 1979).

Kingsbury, J., *Matthew As Story* (2nd edn; Philadelphia: Fortress Press, 1988).

Kloppenborg, J. S., *The Formation of Q: Trajectories in Ancient Wisdom Collections* (Philadelphia: Fortress Press, 1987).

McGrath, A., *A Passion for Truth: The Intellectual Coherence of Evangelicalism* (Leicester: Apollos, 1996).

Mack, B. L., *A Myth of Innocence: Mark and Christian Origins* (Philadelphia: Fortress Press, 1988).

Marshall, I. H., *Luke: Historian and Theologian* (Exeter: Paternoster, 1989).

Martin, R. P., *The Epistle of Paul to the Philippians* (Leicester: Inter-Varsity Press, 1959).

Meeks, W., *The First Urban Christians: The Social World of the Apostle Paul* (New Haven/London: Yale University Press, 1983).

Metzger, B. M., *The Text of the New Testament: Its Transmission, Corruption, and Restoration* (rev. edn; Oxford/New York: Oxford University Press, 1968).

Moltmann, J., *The Crucified God* (London: SCM, 1974).

Montefiore, H., *A Commentary on the Epistle to the Hebrews* (London: A. & C. Black, 1964).

Moore, S., *Literary Criticism and the Gospels: The Theoretical Challenge* (New Haven/London: Yale University Press, 1989).

Moore, S., *Poststructuralism and the New Testament* (Philadelphia: Fortress Press, 1994).

Nineham, D., *Saint Mark* (London: Penguin Books, 1963).

Nolland, J., *Luke 18:35 – 24:53* (WBC 35c; Dallas: Word Books, 1993).

Osborne, G. R., 'Redaction criticism' in *Dictionary of Jesus and the Gospels*, ed. J. B. Green and S. McKnight (Downers Grove/Leicester: Inter-Varsity Press, 1992).

Patte, D., *Ethics of Biblical Interpretation: A Reevaluation* (Louisville: John Knox Press, 1995).

Patte, D. and Patte, A., *Structural Exegeses: From Theory to Practice* (Philadelphia: Fortress Press, 1978).

Perrin, N., *What Is Redaction Criticism?* (Philadelphia: Fortress Press/London: SPCK, 1970).

Powell, Mark Allen, *What Is Narrative Criticism?* (Minneapolis: Fortress, 1990).

Rhoads, D. and Michie, D., *Mark As Story: An Introduction to the Narrative of a Gospel* (Philadelphia: Fortress Press, 1982).

Robinson, J. A. T., *The Priority of John* (London: SCM, 1985).

Rowland, C. and Corner, M., *Liberating Exegesis: The Challenge of Liberation Theology to Biblical Studies* (London: SPCK/Louisville: John Knox Press, 1990).

Ruether, R. Radford, *Sexism and God-Talk: Towards a Feminist Theology* (London: SCM, 1983).

Sanders, E. P. and Davies, M., *Studying the Synoptic Gospels* (London: SCM/Philadelphia: Trinity Press International, 1989).

Schmidt, K. L., *Der Rahmen der Geschichte Jesu* (1919 [never translated]).

Schnackenberg, R., *Jesus in the Gospels: A Biblical Christology* (Louisville: John Knox Press, 1995).

Schneiders, S. M., *The Revelatory Text: Interpreting the New Testament as Sacred Scripture* (San Francisco: HarperCollins, 1991).

Schüssler Fiorenza, E., *In Memory of Her: A Feminist Theological Reconstruction of Christian Origins* (rev. edn; London: SCM, 1994).

Schweitzer, A., *The Quest of the Historical Jesus* (3rd edn; London: A. & C. Black, 1954).

Seeley, D., *Deconstructing the New Testament* (Leiden: Brill, 1994).

Streeter, B. H., *The Four Gospels: A Study of Origins* (rev. edn; London: Macmillan, 1951 [1924]).

Talbert, C. H., *Reading Luke* (London: SPCK/New York: Crossroad, 1982).

Theissen, G., *The Social Setting of Pauline Christianity* (Minneapolis: Fortress Press/Edinburgh: T. & T. Clark, 1982).

Thiselton, A. C., *New Horizons in Hermeneutics* (London: HarperCollins/Grand Rapids: Zondervan, 1992).

Trible, P., *God and the Rhetoric of Sexuality* (Philadelphia: Fortress Press, 1978/London: SCM, 1992).

Trible, P. *Texts of Terror: Literary-Feminist Readings of Biblical Narratives* (Philadelphia: Fortress Press, 1984).

Vermes, G. (ed.), *The Dead Sea Scrolls in English* (3rd edn; London: Penguin Books, 1990 [1987]).

Watson, F. (ed.), *The Open Text: New Directions for Biblical Studies?* (London: SCM, 1993).

Weber, M., *The Theory of Social and Economic Organization* (New York: Glencoe, 1947).

Wellhausen, J., *Prologomena zur Geschichte Israels* (1878 [never translated]).

Whybray, R. N., *The Making of the Pentateuch* (Sheffield: JSOT Press, 1987).

Würthwein, E., *The Text of the Old Testament* (London: SCM/Grand Rapids: Eerdmans, 1979).

Young, E. J., *An Introduction to the Old Testament* (Grand Rapids: Eerdmans, 1964).

Young, F. W., *The Art of Performance* (London: Darton, Longman and Todd, 1990).

Young, F. W., 'Allegory and the ethics of reading' in *The Open Text,* ed. F. Watson (SCM, 1993), pp. 103–20.

Index of Bible references

General index